Mahmoud Dhaouadi was born in a rural region called Zreeba near the towns of Kalaat al-Andalus and Aousdja in the northeast of Tunisia where no formal school existed. His father established the Qutab (a place for learning the Quran and writing and reading Arabic) to teach his children. Mahmoud studied his secondary education in the Zeituna school where Arabic is the single teaching language of all subjects, unlike most of the other Tunisian schools. His higher education was in USA and Canada where he received a BA in psychology and an MA and Ph.D. in sociology. He taught at worldwide universities. Professor Dhaouadi has published over 20 interdisciplinary books, over 200 essays, long and short articles, and book reviews, in Arabic, English, and French.

To Ibn Khaldun, an interdisciplinary social scientist in the 14th century.

Mahmoud Dhaouadi

HUMANS AS THIRD DIMENSIONAL BEINGS

Within Social Science and Islamic Perspectives

AUSTIN MACAULEY PUBLISHERS™

LONDON • CAMBRIDGE • NEW YORK • SHARJAH

Ordering Information
Quantity sales: Special discounts are available on quantity purchases by corporations, associations, and others. For details, contact the publisher at the address below.

Publisher's Cataloging-in-Publication data
Dhaouadi, Mahmoud
Humans as Third Dimensional Beings

ISBN 9781649797445 (Paperback)
ISBN 9781649797452 (ePub e-book)

Library of Congress Control Number: 2023921509

www.austinmacauley.com/us

First Published 2024
Austin Macauley Publishers LLC
40 Wall Street, 33rd Floor, Suite 3302
New York, NY 10005
USA

mail-usa@austinmacauley.com
+1 (646) 5125767

Colleagues who have supported the book's new ideas in
cultural sociology.

Table of Contents

Chapter V: 'The Third Human Dimension' Paradigm: A New Intellectual Framework for the Promotion of Cultural Sociology   **149**

Preface

The Missing Homo Culturus in Social Sciences

The concept of Homo Culturus is *missing* in contemporary social sciences. Economists and those who have a materialist view have described man as Homo Oeconomicus, political scientists have labeled him/her as Homo Politicus and sociologists see the human being as a social being or Homo Sociologus. Because of the present increasing use of numbers today, some have called humans as Homo Numericus. Furthermore, contemporary anthropologists have followed suit despite their great interest in the study of culture; they have *not* used terms related to culture to describe Man as first of all *a Homo Culturus*. Positivism's epistemology has been dominant in social sciences. Its impact is strongly present among leading anthropologists. In his book *The Concept of Culture 1973:26*, Leslie White mentions that Ralph Linton, Radcliffe-Brown, and others considered culture *an abstraction* or *it does not exist* or it designates *no concrete reality*. Positivists are not friendly to *the invisible* and *the innate factors* which influence behaviors. This should explain those anthropologists' attitudes toward culture.

The above reserved attitude to culture is also felt among *The Founding Fathers* of Western sociology. The pre-1960 theorists of culture like Weber, Durkheim, Marx, Parsons, Mills, and others are known to have had a *'weak program'* in their published works. That is, *they gave culture minor importance*. Furthermore, the Birmingham School, Bourdieu, Foucault have not done better: they have adopted a 'weak program' in the study of culture. The 'weak program' trend still dominates sociological studies of culture today even though the *'strong program'* (giving culture great importance) of cultural sociology has gained more attention since the birth of the so-called *'cultural turn'* in the late 1990s.

My research has *incidentally* led me to have a long friendship with the study of culture. My intellectual curiosity in the 1990s motivated me to try to work out a *theoretical framework* that would help understand and explain people's behaviors and the dynamics of human societies. In his book *The Art of Social Theory* 2014, sociologist Richard Swedberg argues that sociological theorizing is not in good standing. I felt I should take the risk in the theorizing adventure. I began by raising this *methodological question*: where should I start to explore the puzzle of the forces behind human behaviors and the dynamics of societies? I thought I must start first by identifying *the special traits* that distinguish *the human species* from the rest of the species. I believe that those traits should put my research to *square one.* In pursuit of potential distinctive human traits, I left no stone unturned to finally discover what I was looking for: *Cultural Symbols/CS*: (language, thought, knowledge, religion, laws, myths, cultural values, and norms). Thus, the study of CS is *very basic* for the understanding and explanation of human behaviors and societal phenomena. My theorizing insight has led me to look at language as the compelling force for the birth of CS: Language is *the Mother* of CS. That is, the human being is not only a speaking animal as described by ancient philosophers and social thinkers, but she/he is also a great user of CS. As such, my Cogito would state: *I use language, therefore, I am human.*

These theoretical assumptions have led to *field observations* which strongly reinforce the concept of *Homo Culturus*. I found four distinct human features which can explain why humans are Homo Culturus.

The centrality of the CS in the human identity may be considered *new* in contemporary social sciences, as outlined. My conceptualization of CS in the core of human identities (Homo Culturus) was reached as follows:

1. The process of the human body's growth and maturation is *slow* compared with those of most other living beings. For instance, on average human babies begin walking at the age of one year, while animal babies may walk right away or within a few hours or days after their birth.
2. Humans have a *longer lifespan* than most animals.
3. The human race has an uncontested *dominant role* on the planet.
4. Humans are *privileged* by CS.

The human identity is made up of two parts: *the body and CS*. It is fully a bi-dimensional identity which is often referred to in religions and philosophy as a dual identity made of body and soul.

The slow human body growth and maturation constitute *two fronts* of human existence: the body and CS fronts. So, humans are *bi-dimensional* in their global development. In contrast, the growth and maturation of non-human species are largely *uni-dimensional* (body) because of their lack of CS in the broad and sophisticated human sense. The process of two levels is seen to be behind the human slow body growth and maturation. That is, the process of the human body growth and maturation is slowed down, so to speak, because humans are involved in a *second process* of growth and maturation represented by CS. CS should answer the question on the cover of the Special Issue of *Scientific American* (September 2018): "Humans: Why we are *unlike* any other species on the planet." As pointed out, Humans are distinctive by CS from other species. Thus, CS makes them unlike other species. It has just been outlined that CS can explain the four distinctive human features. CS can explain countless specific special behaviors of human individuals and groups as well as the variety of dynamics of societies and civilizations. Thus, CS is compatible with *The Principle of Parsimony*: The use of the lowest possible number of variables in order to explain the maximum possible number of phenomena. The following six chapters of this book shed light in details and in some depth on the ideas mentioned in this preface.

Chapter I
The Rise and Meaning of the
Third Human Dimension

The Birth of the Third Human Dimension

Following my return to Tunisia, my home country, after my studies and teaching in North America as well as other countries, I began my serious course of thinking and research in attempting to build a sort of *paradigm* in order to understand human nature and the dynamics of human societies within the perspectives of sociology and psychology, which are the two disciplines of my higher education specialization. I adopted the next steps in order to attempt to fulfill that goal:

1. My intellectual curiosity has proposed to me and encouraged me to work out a coherent intellectual framework based on sociological and psychological insights that help understand and explain people's behaviors and the movements of societies and civilizations. I told myself with adequate trust and optimism that what I am looking for *was not an impossible one*.

2. I continued my dialogue with myself with courage raising this methodological question: where should I start to explore the puzzle of human nature and societal dynamics? My answer to this question has expressed itself this way: I must begin first by identifying *the special traits* that distinguish the human species from the rest of the other species. Because I saw that the discovery of those traits puts the course of my research on good

grounds at *square one*. I strongly believe that these traits are very suitable for a credible trustworthy understanding and explanation of people's behaviors and the dynamics of human societies.

3. I have found fit for this what I call *the third human dimension/ THD/culture* (language, thought, knowledge, religion, laws, myths, cultural values, and norms) which distinguish the human species from the rest of the species. The naming of this dimension as *a third one* of human nature qualifies well, given that human entities are made—according to my own conceptualization—of *three features* (body, soul, and THD). Thus, it has become clear to me that the profound study of the THD is the crux of the matter for the understanding and explanation of human behaviors and societal phenomena. Consequently, my writings are influenced to a great degree by the impact of the idea of the concept/theory of the THD. My newly published English, French, and Arabic books are examples of this (Dhaouadi 2013, 2010).

4. Then I asked: which element of the third human dimension is *the decisive and crucial one* in the making of the entire THD system among humans? The answer to this question is found to be language in its spoken and written forms. Thus, I describe *language as the Mother of all components making the THD.*

This gives legitimacy to call the human being *a linguistic-cultural being* by nature. That is, the human being is not only a speaking being as described by ancient philosophers and social thinkers but he/she is also at the same time a great user of the components of the THD. Based on what has already been underlined, one can imitate Descartes' Cogito and state: *I use language, therefore, I am human.* In other words, humans acquire the unique characteristics of being human with the full third human dimension qualities by the use of the gift of language in both forms.

Following the above four thoughtful observations, I come now to the substance of certain ideas that enforce the thesis of the THD. These ideas have allowed me to establish *a theoretical perspective* for the concept of the THD. The perspective is based on a set of somewhat innovative and unusual personal research observations on five features that distinguish the human species from the rest of the species.

Basic Observations on Human Distinctiveness

My present cultural thesis (humans are cultural symbolic beings (THD) by nature: Humanity as Homo Culturus) is based on *a set of five observations/concepts*. To my knowledge, the centrality of THD in the human identity, as illustrated in the drawing below, may utterly be *new and innovative* in contemporary social sciences. Here is how I have been led to develop this fresh conceptualization of the centrality of culture in human identities (Homo Culturus):

1. The process of the human body's growth and maturation is *very slow* compared with those of other living beings. For instance, on average human babies begin walking at the age of one year, while animal babies may walk right away or within a few hours or days after their birth.
2. In general, humans have *longer lifespan* than most animals.
3. The human race has an uncontested *dominant role* on this planet.
4. Humans are privileged by the THD.
5. In my own conceptualization, the human identity is made up of three parts: the body, the soul, and the THD. Thus, it is fully a *tri-dimensional identity* which is often referred to in religions and philosophy as a dual identity made of body and soul.

The THD Insightful Explanation

The slow human body growth and maturation could be accounted for by the fact that human global growth and maturation involve *two fronts*: The body front and that of the THD. In short, the growth and maturation of non-human species are *uni-dimensional* (body) because of their lack of the THD in the most complex human sense of the term. In contrast, the growth and maturation of humans are *bi-dimensional*. They involve two levels: the body level and the THD level. So, this process of two levels is seen by this author to be behind the human slow body growth and maturation. That is, the process of the human body growth and maturation is slowed down, so to speak, among humans because humans are involved in *a second process* of growth and maturation represented by the THD. This interpretation has *an insightful quality* and certainly a lot of *novel spirit* which are more likely to promote its scientific credibility. To my knowledge, I have never come across this idea in the literature of contemporary social sciences: why the walking of human babies is *delayed* compared with that of animal babies and how the THD/*culture* can offer a sound explanation for this phenomenon. The following drawing describes the central position and role of the THD in the making of the human identity.

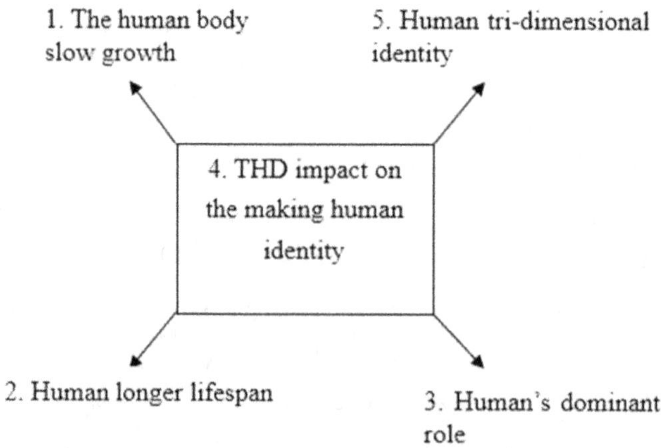

The THD Marginality in Social Sciences

There is almost total silence on the THD in contemporary social sciences. Economists and those who have a materialist view have described man as Homo Oeconomicus. On their part, political scientists and those interested in political issues have labeled man as Homo Politicus. As to sociologists, they see the human being as a very social being or Homo Sociologus. Because of the present increasing use of numbers today, some have called man a Homo Numericus (Compiègne 2011). However, despite their great interest in the study of culture, contemporary anthropologists have not used terms related to culture to describe man as first of all *a Homo Culturus* (White 1973). This marginalization of the importance of culture and its central and decisive role in helping to understand and explain human phenomena is a marginalization that is likely to damage the credibility of these social sciences. It could be argued that social sciences can hardly secure theoretically and empirically good understanding and explanation of human and social phenomena without giving a central role to culture in their making.

Man: The Non-Homo Culturus

The Special issue of the French Review Science & Avenir (Jan–Feb 2012) has asked 100 eminent scientists from natural as well as social sciences the following question: Qu'est-ce que l'Homme? What is Man? None of the answers has provided a definition of man as first of all a cultural being. The answer of the French sociologist Edgar Morin is no exception. Because of his great interest in the complexity of phenomena, Morin labels man as Homo Complexus (p.62).

The negligence of the major importance of culture is hardly new in Western social sciences. The pre-1960 theorists of culture like Weber, Durkheim, Marx, Parsons, Mills, Communists, Fascists, and others are known to have had a 'weak program' for the importance of culture in their published works. In other words, *they gave culture minor importance* in their analysis (Semashko, Daloz, Erdemir 2006:831–838). Furthermore, the Birmingham School, Bourdieu, Foucault, and the theory of production and consumption of culture have not done better on their part: they have adopted a 'weak program' in the study of culture.

The 'weak program' trend *still dominates sociological studies of culture* today even though the 'strong program' (giving culture a first importance) of cultural sociology is gaining more attention, especially among American sociologists since the birth of the so-called 'cultural turn' in the late 1990s (Wolff 1999:503).

The 'weak program' that sociologists have adopted for the study of culture may be explained, in part, by what Alain Touraine considers sociologists' negligence to focus on *social actors*. Touraine claims that sociologists tend to be interested in the study of systems like industrial and capitalist societies. He argues that contemporary thought has minimized *the subjective side of social actors* as Marx, Freud, and Nietzsche had done (Wieviorka 2007:25–27). Touraine stresses the importance for *social sciences to combine the social system and the social actors* in their analysis to understand and explain social action in society, "It is neither excessive nor paradoxical to say that the idea of society is a major obstacle which bothers the development of social sciences because they are based on the separation and even the opposition between the system and the social actors, while the idea of society implies their direct link." (Wieviorka 2007:28).

References

Compiègne, I. (2011) *La société numérique en question(s),* Auxerre Cedex, Editions Sciences Humaines.

Dhaouadi, M. (2013a) *Cultural Sociology within Innovative Treatise: Islamic Insights on Human Symbols*, Lanham, University Press of America Inc.

Introduction to Cultural Sociology (in Arabic) Beirut, Majd publisher 2010.
L'univers des symboles humains: L'Autre sous-développement au Maghreb et au Tiers-monde, Tunis, L'Or du temps, 2010.

Science et Avenir magazine, Jan–Feb. 2012.

Semashko, L. and others (2006) *International Sociology Review of Books*,**2**,6, 829–38.

Wieviork, M. (ed.2007) *Les sciences sociales en mutation*, Auxerre Cedex, Editions Sciences Humaines.

White, L. (1973) *The Concept of Culture*, Edina, MN, Alpha Editions.

Wolff, J. (September 1999) 'Cultural Studies and the Sociology of Culture,' *Contemporary Sociology*, 28, 5, 499–506.

Chapter II
Man: The Homo Culturus

The Chapter's Goal

To further explore the ideas underlined in the proceeding pages, this chapter wishes to explore the legitimacy of calling *Man a Homo Culturus/ a THD being*. I have found an almost total silence on this in contemporary social sciences. Economists and those who have a materialist view have described man as Homo Oeconomicus. On their part, political scientists and those interested in political issues have labeled man as Homo Politicus. As to sociologists, they see the human being as a very social being or Homo Sociologus. Because of the present increasing use of numbers today, some have called man a Homo Numericus (Compiègne 2011). However, despite their great interest in the study of culture, contemporary anthropologists have not used terms related to culture to describe man as first of all *a Homo Culturus* (White 1973). This marginalization of the importance of culture and its central and decisive role in helping to understand and explain human phenomena is a marginalization that is likely *to damage the credibility* of these social sciences. It could be argued that social sciences can hardly secure theoretically and empirically good understanding and explanation of human and social phenomena without giving a central role to culture in their making. Such a marginalization can be explained by social scientists' lack of doing *Basic Research* on many *forgotten dimensions* and *their intrinsic nature* of what I have called the THD: spoken and written language, thought, religion, knowledge/science, myths, laws, cultural values and norms, as it will be shown in this chapter.

It can be said that modern social sciences have not paid greater attention to the most important features (CS/ THD) in the human identity, but they have rather given almost their entire interest to less central dimensions of Man's identity (sex, economics, politics, sociability, etc.). In other words, the thought of these social sciences may be described as a thought that has given a priori attention to what is close to the important instead of giving their entire attention to *the most important dimensions* in Man and society which are represented by the THD (Dhaouadi 2006:28) as claimed by this book's chapters.

Man: The Non-Homo Culturus

As already underlined, the special issue of the French review Science & Avenir (Jan–Feb 2012) has asked 100 eminent scientists from natural as well as social sciences the following question: Qu'est-ce que l' Homme? What is Man? None of the answers has provided a definition of man as first of all a cultural being. The answer of the French sociologist Edgar Morin is no exception. Because of his great interest in the complexity of phenomena, Morin labels man as Homo Complexus

The negligence of the major importance of the THD/culture is hardly new in Western social sciences. The pre-1960 theorists of culture like Weber, Durkheim, Marx, Parsons, Mills, Communists, Fascists, and others are known to have had a 'weak program' for the importance of culture in their published works. In other words, *they gave culture minor importance* in their analysis (Semashko, Daloz, Erdemir 2006:831–838). Furthermore, the Birmingham School, Bourdieu, Foucault, and the theory of production and consumption of culture have not done better on their part: they have adopted a 'weak program' in the study of culture. The 'weak program' trend still dominates sociological studies of culture today even though the 'strong program' (giving culture a first importance) of cultural sociology is gaining more attention, especially among American sociologists since the birth of the so-called 'cultural turn' in the late 1990s (Wolff 1999:503). There is wide consensus that American anthropologist Clifford Geertz has launched the 'strong program' (SP) for the study of culture. The two axioms of the SP are the autonomy of culture and the cultural textuality of social life. That is, *culture is life's internal text.*

As mentioned before, the 'weak program' that sociologists have adopted for the study of culture may be explained, in part, by what Alain Touraine considers sociologists' negligence to focus on *social actors.* Touraine claims that sociologists tend to be interested in the study of systems like industrial and capitalist societies. He argues that contemporary thought has minimized *the subjective side of social actors* as Marx, Freud, and Nietzsche had done (Wieviorka 2007:25–27). Touraine stresses the importance for *social sciences to combine the social system and the social actors* in their analysis to understand and explain social action in society, "It is neither excessive nor paradoxical to say that the idea of society is a major obstacle which bothers the development of social sciences because they are based on the separation and even the opposition between the system and the social actors, while the idea of society implies their direct link." (Wieviorka 2007:28).

The Making Features of Man – the Homo Culturus

In contrast with the marginal place occupied by culture in the thinking of sociologists underlined above, I would like to emphasize in this chapter that man is profoundly and first of all *a Homo Culturus* before being Homo Oeconomicus, or Homo Politicus or Homo Sociologus. This claim is based on a set of five observations/concepts of my own:

1. The process of the human body's growth and maturation is very *slow* compared with those of other living beings. For instance, on average human babies begin walking at the age of one year, while animal babies can walk immediately after birth or within just a few hours or days after.

2. In general, humans have a *longer* lifespan than those of most of the other animals.

3. The human race has a *dominant role* in this planet.

4. Humans are privileged by what I am calling in this book the THD: spoken and written language, thought, religion, knowledge/science, laws, myths, cultural values and norms…

5. Following the perspective of my assumption that humans are Homo Culturus, the human identity is seen as having two parts: the body and the THD. As such, it is fully *a dualistic identity* which is often referred to in religion and philosophy as an identity made of body and soul.

The Potential Explanation of the Homo Culturus Theory

The slow human body growth and maturation could be accounted for by the fact that *human global growth and maturation involve two fronts*: The body front and that of THD. In short, the growth and maturation of non-human species *are uni-dimensional* (body) because of their lack of THD in the most complex human sense of the term. In contrast, the growth and maturation of humans are *bi-dimensional*. That is, they involve two levels: the body level and the THD level. So, the process of two levels is seen in my hypothesis to be behind the human slow body growth and maturation. This assumption is based on *logical reasoning*. The latter would conclude that the rapid body growth and maturation among non-humans is assumed to be due to the uni-dimensional/body process of growth and maturation. While the slow body growth and maturation among humans is due to the fact that they go through *two processes (body and the THD)* of growth and maturation. In logical reasoning terms, it takes a longer time for the accomplishment of the two processes of growth and maturation to materialize than for just one single process. That is, the process of human body growth and maturation is slowed down, so to speak, among humans because humans are involved in *a second process* of growth and maturation represented by the THD.

The human body growth and maturation peak in the twenties helps to explain *two features of human life*:1. Athletes are known to often retire after they reach the age of 25 years or so. 2. On the intellectual/thought level, humans can hardly manifest mature thinking before the twenties. This could be explained as follows: once humans have finished the business of their body growth and maturation in the twenties, they can now concentrate more, so to speak, on the development and maturation of their THD for the rest of their lives. This should explain as well why real highly mature scientific theories and intellectually complex thought cannot usually see the light before the age of 40 years. Ibn Khaldun's age when he wrote his famous work: *The Muqaddimah* is an example.

The following drawing illustrates *the centrality of the THD* in the human identity. This gives legitimacy to this chapter's cultural perspective/theory which stipulates that humans are by nature cultural symbolic beings or Man is a Homo Culturus. In other words, the THD is at the core of the human race's identity, because it strongly influences/determines the remaining four distinctive human features (1, 2, 3, 5) shown in the drawing below. This makes this theory a very *'strong program'culture-oriented theory*. Since THD/culture is very central to its epistemology, its explanatory perspective, and its theorizing about the behaviors of human individuals and the social dynamics of human societies and civilizations. The theory may, thus, qualify to be an *avant-garde theory* for today's emerging cultural sociology (Spillman 2007).

Drawing

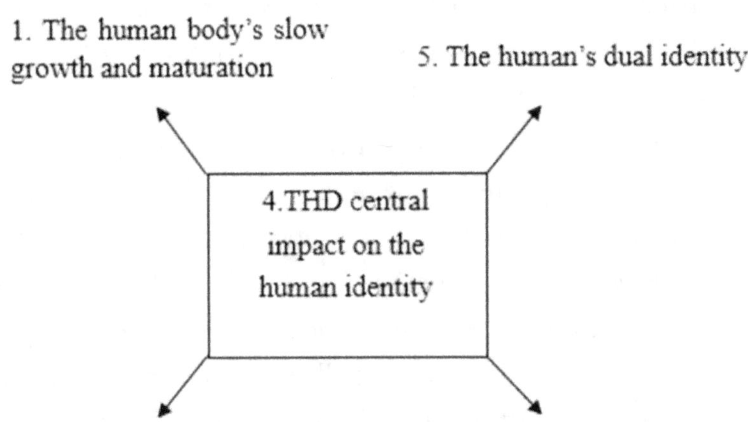

THD's central position in the human entity as shown above leads to the emergence of a new concept that is rather opposite to Sociobiology (Wilson 1975). The new concept is what I would like to call *Culturo-biology*. It means that THD (the human cultural system) has an implicit determinant impact on the very given human body design which is made to be slow in growth and maturation. It is assumed here that the slow body process in question is made so in order to meet the need of THD for a longer human lifespan so they can be fully developed, grown, and matured. This is consistent with the idea of the assumed *influence of mind over matter* or that of the psychological on the organic in humans (Pedler 1981).

The Homo Culturus Theory's Insights

The Homo Culturus theory is labeled also as a *cultural theory* in this chapter. This theory may be considered a fair contribution to the making of both cultural sociology and the 'cultural turn' which has started more than30years ago and has seriously challenged the meta-theoretical assumptions of many classical schools of thought.

Without the study of the THD/culture as a fundamental dimension of human subjectivity, there can hardly be any 'strong program' of sociological analysis of culture. This theory starts its explorations into the world of humans and their societies by considering human social actors as strong THD users by nature. This has required *a thick description* of the THD system which is summarized in *the five new features of the THD*, already mentioned, of which sociologists have generally remained silent. As such, the approach to the study of culture here is *different* from most sociologists. On the one hand, I begin the study of culture as *a distinct basic feature of human nature*. On their part, sociologists study *culture as collective patterns* within societies and civilizations. In other words, my approach in this chapter is made of two steps:

1. 1-The recognition of social actors as strong THD users by nature and the need to understand the inside and outside nature of the THD system. The *thick description of the THD* is, therefore, in order.
2. 2-My perspective explains the impact of the THD on the dynamics of social actors and their societies.

As such, this chapter is an attempt to put forward a *new cultural theory* whose main thesis claims that humans are by nature cultural symbolic beings before being otherwise. In my view, this means that the very deep central core of humans lies at a set of THD which radically distinguish them from the rest of the other living species. My theory strongly states that the system of THD occupies the very center of the human identity which is seen here as being made of THD, on the one hand, and the body dimensions, on the other hand.

Because of its assumed centrality in the human identity, the THD impact on humans is expected to be of a *global nature*. That is, the effects of THD on humans are not limited only to their individual or collective behaviors, emphasized by social scientists, but they are extended as well to *their bio-physiological make-up*.

Consequently, I think that any serious scientific analysis of human political, psychological, economic, and cultural affairs must give first priority to the impact of the THD. The descriptions of man as Homo Politicus, Sociologus, and Oeconomicus can hardly exist and be legitimate and right without the full presence of the THD in the identity of man. As such, THD should be considered the crucial central basis of the making of the very distinguished human nature itself (Dhaouadi 2005:55–66). Thus, the cultural theory presented here should qualify to be an *interdisciplinary general theory* that offers explanations for a variety of human and social phenomena.

My theory strongly belongs to Cultural Sociology and not to the Sociology of Culture, because it considers *culture* an *independent and central variable* in the human identity, something 'hard' and not 'soft' which has a very significant role in human individual behaviors and the social dynamics of human societies. Thus, social scientists must give it a 'strong program' and not a 'weak program' in their theoretical and empirical research. In other words, *culture must be the focus of their study*.

The Missing Inside Nature of Culture

The book of *Cultural Sociology* edited by Lyn Spillman (2007) is considered by many as the best book on the subject. For her, "cultural sociology is about meaning-making. Cultural sociologists investigate how meaning-making happens" (Spillman 2007:1). The book is a reader on cultural sociology made of papers and essays of major sociologists and anthropologists who wrote about culture. Spillman's introduction and her notes on each paper and essay make no mention of the interest of the authors of the selected texts in the study of the *inside/hidden nature* of cultural elements/ the THD. The situation is identical in the book: *The Sociology of Culture* edited by Diana Crane (Crane 1995). This is hardly surprising given the marginal interest in culture among both the founders of the discipline of sociology as well as the prominent sociologists of the twentieth century, as indicated before. So the general silence of sociologists toward the study of the inside nature of culture (INC) is highly expected and predicted.

The following questions tap into what is meant here by the INC: Is culture a material or a spiritual part of humans? Does it have metaphysical/transcendental features? Do cultural elements have a long lifespan and a very strong moving force on the behaviors of individuals and the dynamics of human societies and civilizations? The answers to these questions are dealt with shortly in the main text of this chapter in order to underline a profile of the inside anatomy of the THD.

The lack of the study of the INC is true of Spillman's comments on some very famous scholars in the landscape of culture like Benedict, Shils, Geertz, and Bourdieu. None of them and other cited authors in the book has given first priority to the study of the INC. *Their focus has been rather on* the *external side of culture*. The same thing is also true of the content of the book: *The Sociology of Culture* edited by Crane. Of course, this is consistent with the spirit as well as with the methodology of positivism which was strongly advocated by the founder of Western sociology, August Comte.

A few more basic books on culture are also witness to the lack of interest in INC. *The Concept of Culture* (White1973), *Culture* (Kuper 1999), and *La notion de culture dans les sciences sociales* (Cuche 1996) hardly speak about the INC let alone analyze it and discuss it. This is no surprise given that some anthropologists, for example, have often *a vague idea* about *what culture is*. Ralph Linton asks "Is culture real?" or "Does it exist?" (White 1973), For Radcliffe-Brown, culture is a word that designates no concrete reality but only *an abstraction*, and a very vague abstraction at that. ME Spiro takes a similar position on culture (White 1973:26).

The Epistemological Origin of the Shortcomings

The legitimate question now is this: How could sociologists and social scientists in general study culture in a meaningful way in society and be able to make sound interpretations of cultures or come to solid insights on the meaning-making process without having first *a strong understanding of the INC per se* and its impact on social actors' actions?

The domination of the positivist perspective and that of behaviorism should help to explain the great reservations and skepticism manifested by the social scientists with regard to the inside essence of culture and, subsequently, to its deep inside nature. The heavy impact of *the exclusion* or the marginalization of the recognition and, thus, the study and understanding of the INC has led, on the one hand, to a *later coming* of both sociology of culture and cultural sociology and, on the other hand, to a rather *wide weakness* in many predictions, theories, and paradigms of contemporary social sciences. The increasing interest especially by American sociologists in these two types of sociology should promote the credibility of today's sociology in the West and, consequently, in the East.

Is Theory Building Possible?

The above references to this chapter's *cultural theory* make it appropriate to take a look at the possibility of theory building in social sciences. There are many definitions of the word 'theory' in social sciences. One definition considers a theory a set of concepts and propositions that aim to *explain* a given phenomenon (Dortier 2004:812). Another definition sees a social theory as any attempt to explain facets of social life (*Encyclopedia of Sociology* 1973:274). For hard sciences, "A theory is a general principle supported by a substantial body of scientific evidence which explains observed facts...a theory offers an intellectual framework for future discussion, investigation and refinement" (Bothamley 1993:523).

As to the scientific stand of sociological theories, Turner saw an increasing cynicism about the prospects of the emergence of scientific sociological theories during the last decade of the twentieth century. This was very different around eighty years ago when there was real and great optimism that sociologists would sit at the table of scientists. But today, there *is a much smaller number of sociological theorists* who hold such a position (Turner 2004:30). This attitude on the part of some sociologists is *an anti-science attitude.*

The spirit of real and serious science cannot ethically *deny* the potential progress of science in one field and *advocate* its progress in another. This is plain discrimination in the science orbit by the so-called objective unbiased scientists. Based on this legitimate criticism of some hardcore scientists, sociologists, and other social scientists can fully join the ranks of their fellow hardcore scientists if they improve their scientific research kit in studying the phenomena in their fields. This would allow them to build *credible theories* that can explain individual behaviors as well as the social dynamics of human societies and civilizations.

The negative view toward the scientific stand of the discipline of sociology is not limited to sociologists themselves. Hardcore scientists have a more negative perception of the scientific stand of social sciences at large. In 2000, the journal New Scientist published an editorial on creationism and evolution which *rules out any hope for social sciences* to have credible scientific knowledge on the phenomena they study. The editorial asks: "Will it (science) tell us how to behave toward our fellow humans?" The answer to the editorial is *squarely negative.* For the author of the editorial, science is simply the wrong tool to answer this question and similar ones. In such an attitude, there is an obvious *dehumanization of science.* In a time of globalization, identity crises, environmental concerns, and worldwide fears of modern science hard and software destructive products…how much respect should be accorded to those scientists who *still* do not believe, based on *their false view of things*, that we humans can establish reliable scientific understanding and explanation of human and social phenomena?

Such a position on the part of hardcore scientists and soft (social) scientists displays an extremely *narrow view of science*. This is terribly unacceptable in our time which has been witnessing among scientists and scholars *a growing trend in favor of cooperation between disciplines* (interdisciplinary dialogues) studying phenomena as complex entities with new scientific paradigms that advocate that scientists, researchers, scholars…should be open minded to all types of insights which serve them well in establishing credible and coherent scientific reliable knowledge (Wilson 1999).

The Compelling Legitimacy of Cultural Sociology

Having established that the THD is very central to human identity and is also very distinctive of the human race as a *Homo Culturus/THD* consequently be considered as a *first-class source/reference for social scientists* whose studies attempt to understand and explain the behaviors of individuals as well as the social dynamics of human societies and civilizations. As such, there is a strong legitimacy for cultural sociology to be established, expanded and defended by sociologists. Because this branch of sociology plunges itself deeply into the basic foundation (the THD) of humans and their societies. Unlike other branches of sociology which often deal with peripheral issues in the making of humans and their societies, cultural sociology addresses and focuses its attention deeply on those most fundamental elements (the THD) without which neither humans nor their own societies could come into existence as we have known them as distinct and leading features in this world. Based on this, cultural sociology is strongly qualified to be seen as *the top discipline* not only in the field of sociology but in all other fields of social sciences.

The THD Transcendence

My attempt to deepen the understanding of the profound nature (INC) of the THD has led me to *discover other dimensions* that are hardly outlined, let alone analyzed and discussed in modern social science literature. These new features of THD are expected to enrich and enhance the outlook of cultural sociology. The features in question are:

(a) THD has *neither weight nor volume* in the material sense of the word. That is, the THD does not have a material nature, but it has a rather non-material /transcendental/spiritual nature. Positivist social scientists are very likely to find it strange to use the terms 'weight and volume' when speaking about THD. Nonetheless, neutral objectivity strongly permits the usage of such terms and will give them a lot of meaning. It is sufficient to mention a few examples to make the point:

1) Why do letters and documents sent by fax and e-mail reach their destination much faster than if they were mailed by regular or even rapid mail? The explanation for this, through the concept of weightless and volume less, could be simply put this way: the process of sending letters and documents by e-mail and fax *eliminates* from them the factors of *weight and volume*. This means, that sending by fax and e-mail liberates the sent items from their material parameters (weight and volume) and it returns therefore the THD, so to speak, to their *first initial natural state* referred to as having neither weight nor volume.

With the intrinsic absence of weight and volume in the THD system, it becomes easy to understand why THD can move with high and unbelievable speed through time and space. THD having no material weight and volume may help also explain how it is possible to put the enormous written material of tons of books in a few small electronic flash disks whose weight and volume are too little. This is possible because THD (words of the books in this case) having by their very intrinsic nature no volume and weight *hardly need huge material, vast space* to be contained in it. In philosophical and religious senses, THD belongs to the spiritual and non-material world of humans. THD has its own special characteristics and laws by which it abides and ultimately make them different from *the material world* which has both weight and volume.

2)   The extremely rapid *speed of sound* is another example that is frequently cited. The Concorde plane's fast speed is often compared to that of the sound. This could be explained by the fact that the transmitted word, through the voice-sound at a short distance between individuals or at a far distance during their phone calls, has at its natural state neither weight nor volume. Consequently, the voiced-sent word is naturally predisposed to move with extreme speed, according to the THD perspective being developed and elaborated in this chapter.

3)   Because of their non-material/transcendental nature, the THD is not affected by the reduction factor when we give them to others. For instance, when we give 50 dollars from our capital to others as a charity contribution; this act reduces our capital. But the situation is *quite different* if we give others parts of our thoughts/ideas, knowledge/science, teach them our languages, or spread among them our religious beliefs and cultural symbols.

4)   THD has a longer lifespan throughout time. Ideas, religious beliefs, cultural values, and norms have a long lifespan potential of survival which may last for semi-eternity. *Written and spoken languages* play fundamental roles in the very making of the THD, on the one hand, and their longer lifespan survival, on the other. This is because language is considered in my cultural theory *the Mother of all THD components*. I mean by this, that these components of THD can hardly exist without the human

language in its spoken form at least. As such, one can argue that human language has a potential eternalizing mark/seal that impacts the THD and, thus, makes them strongly qualified to be *spiritual/transcendental*: that is to say, non-material in their very deep essence.

The present outlook on the long lifespan of the THD helps explain the phenomena of the so-called *eternal human thought* of philosophers, scientists, scholars, and religious thinkers of various civilizations since time immemorial. Their thought potential eternity can be accounted for, first, by the use of spoken and written languages which have the eternalizing seal as seen before, and, second, by the fact that *human thought belongs to the transcendental universe of the THD*.

5) The THD can charge humans with fantastic strong energy potentials that enable them to meet and defy the great challenges in human life. In human history, cultural values like freedom, equality, justice, etc.….have proven to charge human individuals, groups, and larger communities with great power that defy the enormous material power of their adversary. As an example, the victory of Third World countries in the twentieth century in their fight for independence from Western colonial occupation is a valid illustration of the imposing role of THD in the liberation of the colonized societies, though they were weaker militarily and materially than their Western occupiers.

Modern social sciences hardly bring up what I call here *transcendental dimensions of culture/ the THD*. There is a continuing widespread silence on these very important dimensions of the THD despite sociologists' increasing interest today in cultural sociology. Our new concepts of Exclusive sociology and Inclusive sociology explain the situation.

From Exclusive Sociology to Inclusive Sociology

The idea of exclusiveness

Probably, the term 'exclusive sociology' has not been used by contemporary sociologists. For us, exclusive sociology is the sociology which *does not like* to pay attention and study certain aspects of individuals and societies because Positivist sociology has *a narrow epistemological view* of things which deprives it from having interest in the so-called *imperceived/non-tangible phenomena*. For example, some anthropologists have argued against the study of culture because it is *an abstaration*/non-tangible. So, they asked: *is culture real*? In his book (*The Concept of Culture*, Leslie White, 1973:26), the author underlines the position of leading anthropologists. Ralph Linton raised the question: *does culture exist*? As to Radcliffe-Brown, he said: *culture* is a word that designates *no concrete reality* but only an abstraction, and *a very vague abstraction*. Another pronouncement is that of M. A. Spiro who says that culture has *no ontological reality*. In other words, culture is not real. Thus, the positivist spirit of this type of anthropology is *exclusive to culture*.

Sociology's exclusiveness of the Other Underdevelopment

Likewise, the main stream sociology of underdevelopment *excludes* the recognition and the study of what we call *'the Other Underdevelopment/OU'*. In dealing with the phenomenon of underdevelopment in the Third World, Western sociologists have tended to confine themselves to the socio-economic and political sides of underdevelopment. The accumulated quantity of Western sociological literature on underdevelopment is impressive. *Yet, there is hardly any reference* to the other sides of underdevelopment (the OU) which we consider as *a psycho-linguistic cultural underdevelopment*. It is a subcategory of the larger phenomenon of the Third World underdevelopment. We measure it by behavioral manifestations like the desire to imitate the West, suffering from inferiority complex, using Western languages like English and French instead of native ones, Third World heavy dependency on Western modern sciences and knowledge and the wide diffusion of Western cultural values in developing countries. Our perspective looks at the OU as having been largely the outcome of Western imperial domination particularly of African and Asian societies.

Behind the Forgotten OU

In response to *this academic and intellectual illiteracy* on the OU, we would like to mention few reasons behind this *Forgotten Underdevelopment*. As expected, one can hardly seek any direct help from Western or Third World Western-oriented sociology in going about defining, conceptualizing and theorizing in this field of research. The sociological illiteracy on the OU needs an explanation. There are several factors behind the missing OU in Western sociology:

1- Emmanuel Wallerstein refers to a general *epistemological reason* which hampers all social scientists from being always objective. The editors of the book (*Public Sociology*, Dan Clawson& al,2007:15) cite Wallerstein as an example: "it is *intrinsically impossible* to keep one's values from entering one's scientific scholarly work."

2- Debates on the discipline of sociology continue at many levels. It is enough to mention few: Michael Burawoy's call for Public Sociology, ISA's invitation for multiple sociologies and Ali Meghji's strong advocacy of the idea of Decolonizing Sociology (mainly Western sociology). These sociological perspectives are against the main stream sociology that embraces *the idea of exclusiveness* of certain phenomena as well as outsider methods and knowledge from the main stream Western sociology.

3- There is a general widespread attitude, especially among Western Liberal sociologists who dealt with development/underdevelopment which *hints or claims* that the cultural heritage (values, traditions, religions, languages.) of underdeveloped societies is largely *an obstacle* to the development process in those countries, Daniel Lerner is an example. This should explain why the OU has no place in his and other studies of modernization/ development in the Third World.

Inclusive Sociology

It is a sociology that takes into account both tangible/material and imperceived/non-material factors which shape individual behaviors and the dynamics of societies. For instance, It rejects the mentioned anthropological exclusion of culture as imperceived/non-tangible. Rather, *culture is a fundamental unique distinctive human feature*. We conceptualize it as a set of non-material /imperceived items: language, thought, religion, science, myths, laws and cultural values and norms. As indicated in previous chapters, we call them *Cultural Symbols/CS/culture*. A scientific question should be raised: why culture is a unique human characteristic? The answer is to be found in something else uniquely human. It is *language* in its spoken and written forms. Humans are the only known species who masters the skill of writing. As to the spoken language, it is widely very different and much superior to means of communication of the non-humans. Thus, there is a strong correlation between human culture and human language as *two unique human phenomena*. So, language is *the Mother of CS* because without it we could hardly imagine the birth of CS/human culture, as spelled out before.

Culture and its transcendental features

Epistemologically, CS/culture has what I call *transcendental characters.* That is, CS is *not of material/tangible nature* unlike the components of the human body and the material world. CS five most important transcendental traits are as mentioned earlier:

1- Because CS nature is not material, it has therefore neither *weight nor volume* in the real sense of the terms.
2- CS enjoys fantastic *rapidity of transmission* over time and space.
3- CS is *undiminished* by sharing unlike elements of the material world. For example, if we give others something from our knowledge, cultural values, and so on we lose nothing.
4- CS has a *great capacity* of *survival* over time particularly through written languages, so CS longevity might be semi-eternal. Languages preserve and immortalize the collective heritage of human communities and the heritage of distinct individuals.
5- CS has *an extraordinary power* to imbue individuals and societies with enormous energy, enabling them to triumph over the greatest challenges. For instance, the values of freedom, justice and equality have been shown, over the long course of human history, to be CS capable of endowing individuals and communities with *colossal, surging energy* similar to overwhelming metaphysical forces which no one can withstand.

Language and the Emergence of Human Culture

Based on the outlook of THD/Homo Culturus theory, it is quite legitimate to look for the *origin of human culture* which distinguishes the human race from the rest of the other species. The human *spoken and written language* appears to be the most likely human factor behind the emergence of the phenomenon of the THD/culture. It is hard to imagine the existence of the remaining elements of the THD system like religion, science, and thought without the presence of the spoken language at least. This is why I consider *language as the Mother of the THD* in my Homo Culturus perspective of analysis of the phenomenon of culture, as outlined previously. Given the central role of spoken and written language in the birth as well as in the making of the THD system/culture as defined by anthropologists and sociologists in particular, it becomes strongly appropriate to endorse the widely cited description of philosophers and social thinkers who have seen *man as a speaking animal*. As such, human language is not only the source on which depends the emergence of human culture, but it is also at the origin of the human race's domination over the rest of the living species through the human sophisticated and complex cultural system.

In spite of language centrality in the human identity and, consequently, in the emergence of the phenomenon of culture/the THD system, the most famous anthropological definition of culture makes, nonetheless, *no explicit mention of language* as central and basic elements of culture, let alone as the major cause for human culture emergence and its making process. The debate on the origin of culture is widely discussed today by social scientists. Though there are small differences between them, yet there is a consensus that *language is the first determining factor* for the emergence of human culture (Dortier: 2005–2006:26–94).

The British anthropologist Edward Bernard Tylor (1871) defined the concept of culture as follows: "Culture or civilization is that complex whole which includes knowledge, belief, art, morals, custom, and any other capabilities and habits acquired by man as a member of society." Tylor's classical definition of culture remains implicitly *silent* on language while it is the constituting and the founding element/force of the phenomenon of culture itself, as just stated. In other words, the *relation between language and culture is of an organic nature*. It is fair to say that Tylor's definition of culture is not fully adequate because of its negligence to clearly include language as part and founding component at the same time for the crystallization of the emergence of culture/ the THD system phenomenon (White 1973). Like Tylor and most social scientists, the French sociologist Bernard Lahire remains silent on the role of language in the making of human culture (Sciences Humaines, October 2023, 362:32–38). He speaks about specificities of the various species. Yet, he does not underline that human spoken and written language is a very specific feature of the human race that has made its very sophisticated culture *specific* to the human species that is described as follows: "Humans: Why we're unlike any other species on the planet" (*Scientific American*, Special Issue, November 2018, 319,3).

The THD and the Making of the Human Mind

The Homo Culturus theory has helped come to *new explanations* of various human phenomena which are hardly raised by researchers, let alone analyzed and explained. For instance, I have found strong relations between THD and human long lifespan, delayed human babies' walk compared with baby animals' quick ability to walk after birth, and the long or semi-eternal presence of human thought after their authors' death. That is, it has been possible for the Homo Culturus theory/ THD to offer genuine explanations for these distinct human phenomena (Dhaouadi 2009:24–46, 2013).

Likewise, I attempt here to shed light on the firm relations that link the THD *to the making of the human mind*, the best feature that distinguishes humans from the rest of the species. In doing so, this reinforces the ability to understand and explain better the THD centrality (Homo Culturus) in the human identity. Consequently, this helps acquire progress and maturation in *theorizing* about single and collective human phenomena based on the THD the most distinguishing factor of humans.

The Human Mind and the THD

When we ask common people: what distinguishes human beings from other living beings? The answer of the majority to this question would be *the human mind*. This answer has a high credibility. Yet, scientific curiosity can hardly be satisfied with this simple answer. It requires knowledge about factors that have led to the presence of the phenomenon of the mind only among humans. In order to have access to the necessary knowledge to explain the human mind phenomenon, the researcher can adopt a transparent systematic methodology made of *three steps*: 1. the search for the possible presence of *other distinct traits* which are also found only among humans, like the mind. 2. In case those distinct traits exist, a plausible hypothesis would follow: there may be a relation between THD and the human mind. 3. A solid assurance of the presence of a link between the human mind and THD will help understand and explain the original roots of the human mind's birth as a very special exclusive human feature.

My continuing research since the 1990s on Man as a Homo Culturus has repeatedly shown *humans are distinct from the rest of the species by the THD set* (Dhaouadi 2009:24–46, 2013). As such, the THD is remarkably *a distinct unique human quality* that satisfies what is required in step1 above. As to the likelihood of the existence of a relation between the human mind and the THD (step 2), this is a plausible hypothesis because *both are unique features of humans*. This allows us to say at least either there is a strong correlation between the two or there is a causality relation between them (step 3).

The situation at hand resembles that of the egg and the chicken: Which comes first?

To elaborate more on the THD-human mind relation issue, we can raise another feature where humans are also unique. *Humans are alone the master of this world*. On the one hand, people attribute this human domination privilege to *the human mind*. On the other, my research indicates that *THD is behind the human mastership in the world* as the above drawing has demonstrated.

Based on what has already been outlined, humans appear to be THD beings by nature. That is, the THD occupies the core of the human identity. Because of the strong link between THD and the human mind, as spelled out, the nature of that link could be clearly identified as *a cause-effect link*. The logic of the assembled observations and, facts as well as the analysis of the intricate relation of the two (the THD and the human mind) allow one to say that humans' possession of the THD set should constitute *the first distinct principal cause* for them to qualify for having the talents of the human mind. Two arguments stand in favor of this: a. The other living beings do not possess the THD. Consequently, they are deprived of the quality of the human mind. b. The impact of THD on the making of human minds can be illustrated in *three types of human minds*: illiterate minds, educated minds, and great-thinking minds, as we will see later.

The THD-Mind Relation Indicators

In order to advance the process of revealing the nature of the relation between the THD and the human mind, it is relevant to make some observations that may help come close to dissipating the vagueness surrounding the THD-mind link in question. Thus, a few examples of some indicators to this link are in order:

1. The skills of reading and learning in schools or independently offer the human mind knowledge and science which enable it to understand and grasp better many things in life. In other words, school teaching makes the mind of the learner more able than the illiterate mind to understand and explain many things in daily life. It is rather clear from this example that the use of certain elements of THD like reading and writing a language and learning some scientific facts, thoughts, and religious and cultural values *improve the ability level of the human mind* in understanding and explaining a number of phenomena and things in its immediate environment at least.

2. The human brain anatomy shows that the frontal cortex is the location for THD such as language and thought and their development and maturation. So, the human mind and the THD are *two distinct features of humans* which could suggest the hypothesis of the presence of a possible strong relation between

the two. This hypothetical link is epistemologically fit to consider *the THD as the first source* for the making of the phenomenon of the human mind among the members of the human race. As such, *the absence of THD* among the other living species, as mentioned, has deprived them of having the characteristics of the human mind. As such, it is rather difficult to speak of the existence of the human mind without the presence of the THD. In other words, man as a human being uses very widely the THD which explains the phenomenon of *three kinds of the human mind*: illiterate minds, educated minds, and *great-thinking minds*. I focus now on the roots and nature of the last type of human mind.

The Determinants of Great Minds

A sociology of knowledge is needed to explore and identify the basic factors behind the making of great creative human minds in the domain of human knowledge (1) *Three fundamental factors* appear to be strongly correlated with the presence of brilliant human minds. These are (a) wide knowledge, (b) stimulating external milieu, and (c) special human personality traits.

I focus here on the first factor (a) by analyzing *Ibn Khaldun's great intellectual mind* as a case study. The second factor's impact (b) on Ibn Khaldun's new creative social thought has already been over studied and discussed by those who attempted to understand and explain the roots of his *New Social Science Thought* (Ilm al-umran al-bashari). As to the personality traits factor (c), it seems to be the least studied, though it may be so important for winning the realization of human creativity (Dhaouadi 1998:23–48). Given this chapter's limited space, it does not allow us to deal with it (c) in any meaningful way. However, colleagues and readers may like to consult my modest work both in English and Arabic on the role of Ibn Khaldun's personality traits in the making of his pioneering social thought. (Dhaouadi, 2004:54–63, 2001:66–82, 1997:85–97) There has been a controversy among researchers and scholars on the real science of the phenomenon of creativity (Discover, 1996, Sternberg 1999, Simonton 2012:35–41). Thus, the safest way is to look at creativity as the result of the interaction of those three factors where the input of each one of them is not necessarily equal to the two others.

However, the main focus of this section of this chapter is *twofold*. First, to shed light with analysis and discussion on how Ibn Khaldun's Islamic wide knowledge had shaped his cognitive worldview/Weltanschauwing and, consequently, his imposing intellectual social science mind. Second, to assess and evaluate the credibility in the field of knowledge-making of what is called in the Muslim culture *'the Aql-Naql Mind'* which combines revealed knowledge with human reasoning made knowledge in the process of knowledge acquisition and creation. Both cases (wide knowledge and Aql-Naql knowledge) are ultimately the result of the THD *repertoire* where knowledge/science and thought are an important part of THD as seen earlier in the definition of the THD. This double focus is in order because it is assumed in this chapter that *wide knowledge is very basic*, on the one hand, for the emergence of great intellectual human minds and that the factors of both stimulating external milieu and special personality traits are considered as essential helping forces to the materialization of great brilliant minds. On the other hand, the THD Aql-Naql mind is hardly acceptable by modern learned Western culture as a means to the establishment of credible knowledge in *the two cultures*. The discussion of this issue is relevant at a time of serious questioning being addressed at the credibility of social and natural sciences, because of *the lack of the epistemological reunification of the two cultures* (Wallerstein, 1999:243, 2001, Wilson, 1999). The Muslim Aql-Naql mind does not only strongly advocate the epistemological unity of the two cultures but also recommends the unity between human-made knowledge and the revealed knowledge.

There is, therefore, a pressing need to get familiar with *Ibn Khaldun's wide scope of knowledge* as well as *his Aql-Naql mind* that have helped prepare him to be the true worldwide pioneer in the entire human history who intelligently and skillfully invented in the fourteenth century the *Science of Human Social Organization* (Ilmu al-umrani al-bashari/Sociology).

Knowledge and Creativity

Throughout humankind's long history and its diverse cultures and civilizations, the emergence of great creative minds in various fields of knowledge has often been associated with a good standard of the so-called 'learned advanced knowledge'. This requires two basic things: *literacy* and a *high command of knowledge* in one's field in the first place. However, the literacy factor may not be necessary for innovation and creativity in certain fields of human activities. But literacy is very fundamental for creative and innovative minds in most of the branches of human knowledge. That is, *literacy* is a necessary tool for the unfolding and expansion of the corpus of human science and knowledge as a significant feature of THD. Theories in the field of creativity highlight the relationship between creativity and knowledge. (Sternberg, 1999:226–250, 2003) Those theories stress the rather straight forward relation between the two (Sternberg, 1999:248). Because it is assumed by theorists of creativity that the more one knows, the easier it will be to develop innovative solutions (Kraft, 2005:22). *Wide knowledge* initiates also intense complex cognitive processes which may often lead to moments of brilliance among humans (Kraft, 2005:17).

This may be a hasty conclusion because it minimizes the role of the two mentioned other factors involved in the creativity process. Despite this caution, the relation between Ibn Khaldun's wide THD Islamic knowledge background and his creative new social science remains a testing ground in this chapter for those theories. *Creativity* standard definition is 'people's ability to go beyond given information and imagine new and exciting ways of reformulating old problems' (Sternberg, 2003: I).

Ibn Khaldun's Education and Knowledge

In his youth in Tunis, Ibn Khaldun studied *three main areas:*

> (1) Islamic studies, which covered the science of the Quran, the Hadith (the Prophet's sayings and behaviors) as well as Islamic jurisprudence (Fikh), especially of the Malikite School; (2) the sciences of the Arabic language which deal with the grammar, conjugation and the art of eloquent written and spoken language (al-Balaga) and (3) logic, philosophy, natural sciences and mathematics. This shows that Ibn Khaldun had an educational background in the two cultures of his time. In his autobiography book *At-Ta'rif bi-Ibn Kaldun warihlatuhu gharban wa sharqan* (Information about Ibn Khaldun and His Travel in the West and the East of the Arab World) [2], he describes in detail two of his most distinguished educated teaching scholars. They are Abu Muhammad ibn Abd al Muhaymin al-Hathrami and Abu Abd Allah Muhammad al-Abilly (Al-Ta'rifA:21–23, F:47–49). Ibn Khaldun speaks of al-Hathrami as the Moroccan leading scholar in the sciences of grammar and Hadith. He received fundamental knowledge from him on *the six reference books* on Hadith and other important books on the subject like al-Muwattaa, the reference book of the famous Malikite jurisprudent and theologian (Faqih) Maalik Ibnu Anas.

As to his second master, *al-Abilly,* he taught Ibn Khaldun the two fundamental sciences (al-asliyyayni): logic and all philosophical and mathematical disciplines. Al-Abilly found Ibn Khaldun well-talented in those subjects *(At-Ta'rif, A:23, F:49).* Ibn Khaldun himself admits he had a strong desire for learning and knowledge since his early infancy:

"Since my very early infancy, the time of my weaning, I have never ceased to seek knowledge and the best virtues, dividing my time between attending the courses and the circles of scholars until the time of the devastating plague that killed dignitaries, notables and most of my teachers in Tunis. Consequently, most scholars and writers who were not affected by the plague left for Morocco." (*At-Ta'rif*, A:57, F:72).

Ibn Khaldun had later the opportunity to return to his studies in Fez which became the center of scholars and writers who immigrated from Al-Andalus (Spain) and Tunisia. Fez had the greatest Islamic libraries. Ibn Khaldun's presence in this stimulating intellectual learned milieu has expanded and consolidated his scope of knowledge and satisfied his true desire for knowledge. He writes:

"I took advantage of the situation to reflect and read and meet the great scholars from Morocco and Al-Andalus who came as ambassadors of their princes to the Moroccan sultan. I thus, fulfilled my desire for the acquisition of knowledge" (*At-Ta'rif*, A:61, F:75).

Ibn Khaldun's Praised Mind

The mentioned educational background of Ibn Khaldun in various sciences of *the two cultures* (as part of the THD repertoire) had its impact on the shaping of his intellectual mind. There has been an overwhelming worldwide consensus among intellectuals and scholars that Ibn Khaldun is blessed with a great mind. From the West, the British famous historian, Arnold Toynbee spoke about Ibn Khaldun's mind this way:

"He (Ibn Khaldun) has conceived and formulated a philosophy of history which is undoubtedly *the greatest work of its kind* that has ever been created by any mind in any time and place" (Toynbee, 1956:372).

From the East, the late well-known Moroccan intellectual and Ph. D. author of Ibn Khaldun's thought sees the *Muqaddimah* as "A *pyramidical and unified construct and developed thought* in its content as well as in the organization of its chapters, paragraphs and the harmony which prevails among its various parts" (Al-Jabri, 1982:118–19).

The Muslim Mind's Ethics of Knowledge

In order to understand the specific nature of Islamic-wide knowledge factors (as part of THD repertoire) that shaped Ibn Khadun's intellectual mind, we need to look at the main general characteristics of the Muslim intellectual mind, since it is assumed, from a sociological perspective, that Ibn Khaldun's intellectual mind had worked out his New Science (ilmal-umran al-bashari) within *the religious cultural framework setting* of the Muslim intellectual mind before Western domination and colonization of the Islamic world in the contemporary period. The Muslim classical intellectual mind was heavily influenced by *the Quran's ethics toward knowledge acquisition and creation.* The ethics could be summarized in the following features:

1) The Quran gives top priority to knowledge acquisition and creation. The first revealed Quranic verses strongly stress the importance of literacy and continuing learning to secure wide knowledge of everything in this world/universe.

2) In order to seek knowledge as well as to develop it, the Quranic text asks Muslims as well as non-Muslims to adopt the methodology of continuing observations of three main areas: (a) the universe/nature, (b) the historical events of human civilizations, societies, and their social actors and (c)the human distinct nature. This Quranic appeal certainly serves well for the development of the sciences of the two cultures. *The epistemological unity* of the latter comes from the Quranic idea of *the one God*, the only creator of all world/universe phenomena which the sciences of the two cultures study.

3) In the Quranic view, true authentic knowledge should make scientists/scholars the most pious and humble people toward God 'Among his Servants are those who have knowledge' (The Quran: 35:28). From the Islamic perspective, the achievement of good credible knowledge is a spiritual salvation act for true

scientists and scholars. This is in significant contrast with the view of the modern Western mind in the two cultures.

4) Regardless of how enormous and vast, human knowledge always remains very limited compared with God's unlimited and fully global and certain knowledge.

5) The divine knowledge has absolute authenticity, certainty, and inclusiveness of all things in the world and the universe at large.

The Cognitive THD Aql-Naql Muslim Mind

It is clear from the previous short biographic and autobiographic sketches and the profile of the THD learning Muslim mind that Ibn Khaldun's education and learning backgrounds as well as the societies he studied were profoundly *Islamic* in nature.

On the one hand, he had a wide and high standard of knowledge of the various Islamic THD sciences and disciplines (the two cultures) of his time as shown in the Sixth Part of his Muqaddimah. On the other hand, Ibn Khaldun had first-hand experience and knowledge about numerous Arab Muslim societies, tribes, clans, and groups he analyzed and wrote about with his Umran mind. In other words, his social theoretical and field work THD knowledge are Islam-inspired. Thus, Ibn Khaldun's intellectual mind is bound to be heavily a Muslim mind which is the outcome both of the Islamic THD learned culture and that of the social realities of the Muslim Arab societies. *Gibb's description* of Ibn Khaldun's thought leaves no doubt about his Muslim identity as a great thinker:

'Ibn Khaldun was not only a Muslim, but as almost every page of the Muqaddimah bears witness, a Muslim jurist and theologian, of the strict Maliki school. For him, religion was far and away the most important thing in life. The Sharia is the only true guide' (Shaw, Polk, 1962:171).

On his part, the author Al-Shaqaa affirms that Ibn Khaldun's Umran Theory is Islamic from the beginning to the end. (Al-Shaqaa, 1992:100–130). Ibn Khaldun himself appears to be referring to his authentic

Islamic and personal thought when he denies the foreign influence on the conceptualization of his new science:

"We became aware of these things with God's help and without the instruction of Aristotle or the teachings of the Mobedhan" (Dawood,1974:41).

The Islamic culture/ THD features of Ibn Khaldun's mind are furthermore manifested in what we may call *the cognitive Aql-Naql perspective* of the Muslim mind.

Historically speaking, Arab Muslim civilization's earlier scholars and scientists of all disciplines and sciences (the two cultures) carried out their works on the basis of the principle of *cooperation* between the revealed-sacred knowledge (Naql), on the one hand, and the human-acquired knowledge based on human reason (Aql), on the other. Ibn Khaldun's well-established interdisciplinary social science thought in his Muqaddimah is *no exception* to the rule of the combination of the Naql and Aql knowledge. That is, he strongly adopted *the cognitive dualist (Aql-Naql) perspective* in writing his entire Umran work, including his Muqaddimah. As such, the Khaldunian cognitive mind is well in line with the THD Quranic-inspired five major characteristics of *the ideal type* of the classical intellectual Muslim mind described earlier.

This type of *extremely curious and motivated mind* to learn both from THD Aql and Naql perspectives should help explain the great milestones in many branches of knowledge accomplished by the Arab Muslim civilization before the Middle Ages. Ibn Khaldun's manifested great mind in his Muqaddimah is a convincing example of the potential high intellectual performance of the Muslim THD Aql-Naql mind. This has made me consider this type of mind as *the dividing line* between what I call Khaldunian Eastern Sociology and contemporary Western sociology (Dhaouadi, 1990:319–335). The Khaldunian THD Aql-Naql mind is expected, for instance, to be praised by Wallerstein for *its epistemological unification of the two cultures* in his Muqaddimah (3). But given Wallerstein's Western modern training, it is very difficult for him to take seriously the revealed knowledge part of Ibn Khaldun's

THD Aql-Naql mind since it is against *the academic social norm* of the Western modern mind in knowledge acquisition and creation.

From an Islamic epistemological viewpoint, tensions and conflicts between the THD Aql and Naql parts have *no room* in the Muslim mind. Because the source of the two (Aql and Naql) references is one: Allah. Seen that way *the Muslim mind* could rightly be considered a *meeting ground for the secular and the Revealed knowledge.*

The famous religious scholar Ahmad Ibn Taymiyyah (1263–1328) is the most well-known Muslim learned man who had strongly defended the legitimacy of the promotion of the THD combined Aql and Naql knowledge in the Islamic Culture. His book: *The Prevention of Contradictions between Aql and Naql* is a case in point.

The Two Cultures of the Muslim and Western Minds

The sociological perspective helps understand and explain the differences between these two minds with regard to the acquisition and creation of knowledge. On the one hand, the learned Muslim THD Aql-Naql mind is the outcome of the Muslim culture that sees no contradictions between the THD Aql and Naql knowledge. It emphasizes rather their harmony.

On the other hand, the Western THD learned mind has witnessed a sweeping liberation from the influence of the Christian Theological Thought since the Renaissance. Rational reasoning, experimentation, and the collection of empirical data…have become the only basis for Western THD contemporary knowledge in the two cultures. Al-Jabri sees the difference between these two THD-making minds in the way each one of them classifies in priority the following: *Man, Nature, God.* On the one hand, the Greek European mind gives more importance to the first two. On the other hand, in the Muslim Arab mind priority is given to God and man. This certainly helps account for the non-readiness of the former and the readiness of the latter to adopt the perspective of the THD Aql-Naql mind (Al-Jabri,1988:27–31).

With these THD cultural differences toward knowledge acquisition and creation in perspective, it becomes easy to understand why Westerners have often been impressed by the Aql THD side of Ibn Khaldun's mind and they have denied and criticized him for his use and reference to the THD Naql side (Lacoste, 1998:241–257, Schmit,1999:66–67).

The presence of these two minds in the world of knowledge acquisition and creation makes room for *controversy*. The Western modern THD mind looks with suspicion, disbelief, and even hostility to knowledge colored by religion. In contrast, the classical Muslim THD mind finds support in the fundamental Revealed Islamic texts for human-made knowledge. Furthermore, what may still generate more controversy is that *each one of the two minds has contributed to the advancement of human knowledge*. Since the Western learned THD modern mind is the widely dominant adopted reference for knowledge creation and acquisition in contemporary times, a discussion is appropriate here to see if there is ground or justification for the Muslim THD Aql-Naql mind *to stand on its own feet* and even compete with the Western mind in knowledge acquisition and creation turf.

First, the Muslim THD learned mind is strongly pro-knowledge acquisition and creation. The Quranic text (the first THD Naql source in Islam) is *an open invitation* to Muslims and non-Muslims alike to think and reflect on the world/universe's endless phenomena. It is estimated that the sixth of the Quran's verses speaks directly or indirectly about the importance of THD knowledge of the two cultures for humans. It is in this sense that 'true scientists and scholars are the inheritors of the prophets' according to the Prophet Muhammad (the second Naql source in Islam) who strongly and repeatedly appeals to Muslims to seek knowledge: 'seek knowledge from the cradle to the grave' or 'seek knowledge even in the far distant China'. The knowledge-seeking ethics is, thus, deeply rooted in the Muslim THD Aql-Naql mind.

Second, both the Quranic and the Hadith texts include explicit statements or implicit references to *scientific facts* about various phenomena in the world/the universe which are discovered only recently by modern science. One example from the Quran is sufficient to make the point. The Quranic text has its own terms for the newly developed science of Embryology. It described fourteen centuries ago the specific stages of human fetus development this way:

"We created man from the quintessence of mud, there after We placed him as a drop of liquid (sperm) in a firm lodging (the womb). Then We fashioned the sperm (Nutfah) into something that clings (Alakah) which We fashioned into a chewed-like lump (Muthgha). The chewed-like lump is fashioned into bones which are then covered with flesh. Then, we developed it into another act of Creation. Blessed is God, the best Creator" (the Quran:23/13).

The famous embryologist Keith Moore has strongly praised the Quranic precise terms for the phases of human embryo development (Moore,1982). Furthermore, in his comparative analysis of the place of scientific facts in the Bible and the Quran, the French surgeon Maurice Bucaille comes to *this conclusion*:

"The Quranic statements are in perfect agreement with modern scientific facts which are unconceivable to consider Mohammad as their author. Thus, modern scientific knowledge permits to understand the meanings of certain Quranic verses which are not understood until the present day" (Bucaille,1976:254).

Such scientific credible evidence in favor of the meanings of the Quranic verses can only strengthen the stand of *the THD Aql-Naql cognitive Muslim mind* in the past and the present among Muslims. And it may as well solicit some attention on the part of the modern learned Western mind in the two cultures *to reconsider its negative attitude* toward the validity of knowledge whose source is THD. This may improve the image of Islam particularly in times of crisis between the West and Islam.

Third, it could be argued that the adoption of the THD Aql-Naql mind is also justified because human-made knowledge *always remains problematic*. This type of knowledge is a combination of correctness and error. It is a mixture of certainty and doubt. Man's use of his thoughtful and analytical reasoning often involves *probabilities of truth and falsehood* in the corpus of knowledge he attains. Thinkers, philosophers, and scientists have been, throughout the ages, aware of *the problematic nature* of the correctness/error dimension that characterizes human-made knowledge.

Ibn Khaldun's law of al-Mutabaqa (the correct matching between historical events and human social realities) in the science of history aimed at minimizing the pitfalls of historical knowledge in which Muslim historians were involved before and during Ibn Khaldun's time. This law was meant to raise the level of rightness and credibility in historical knowledge. Something similar could be said as well of the influence of the ethics of positivism and empiricism on modern knowledge. But no doubt, modern knowledge has been and will hardly be able to exhaust all the causes that lead to errors and pitfalls in human-made knowledge. Being limited in scope (in terms of its correctness and certainty in its facts), human-made knowledge would legitimately and modestly need divine knowledge as it is complimentary to help humans deal particularly with controversial ethical, and moral issues that have proven to be rather difficult to settle for the good of Man and society when relying only on human reasoning.

It is clear from the above that the prejudiced Western learned mind against religion is the result of *special socio-historical circumstances* that Western civilization has known since the Renaissance in the confrontation between The Church, on the one hand, and the scientists and Western modernizing societies at large, on the other. This specific Western experience has created among Westerners *a culture of separation and distrust between science and religion*. Thus, they could hardly understand, let alone accept, the cooperation between religion and science as shown in the Aql-Naql Muslim mind. At present, the latter may be getting a boost from two current sources: 1. The beginning of increasing dialogue in the West between religion and science

(Clayton, Simpson 2009) and 2. Getting rather more strength and support from ongoing and future scientific discoveries.

From an Islamic perspective, the Aql-Naql mind is *the ideal mind* to reach out for a more credible and complete solid corpus of knowledge. Ibn Khaldun's Umran mind in his Muqaddimah is an excellent manifestation of the work of the THD Aql-Naql Muslim mind. Ibn Khaldun's Umran mind may be considered the avant-garde of today's *Islamization of knowledge movement.*

This type of mind has not only accomplished a good standard social science handbook (the *Muqaddimah*), but he has achieved, by all objective accounts, *a real breakthrough in the field of social sciences* not only in the Arab Muslim civilization but also in the entire long history of the rest of human civilization. Ibn Khaldun made explicit reference to this:

"In a way, it is an entirely original science. In fact, I have not come across a discussion along these lines by anyone" (Dawood, 1974:39).

Ibn Khaldun's high intellectual pioneering Umran (social science) work raises, therefore, *serious questions* about the assumptions of the modern Western mind's persistent claims that true science and authentic knowledge cannot be obtained if religion and science are not kept separate from each other. As shown, these claims are based on Western knowledge/science and special experience with The Church. Thus, *they ought not to be generalized to other religions' experiences with knowledge creation and acquisition,* Ibn Khaldun's THD Aql-Naql Muslim mind strongly defies the substance of those claims and *opens the lead* for scientists and scholars *to seek more than one way* in order to create and establish solid knowledge in the two cultures.

Conclusion

It is right to raise now this question: why the concept of man as a Homo Culturus/ THD is missing in Western social sciences? For example, it has already been outlined in this chapter that the classical founders of Western sociology had played down the importance of culture in their works. This could be explained by the heavy impact of *the quantitative positivist sociology* on their perspectives as well as their epistemologies. So, culture is marginalized because it pertains mainly to qualitative sociology. *This cultural marginalization* in the social sciences may resemble very much what has happened to the natural sciences in their study of the human brain. The latter is conceived by biologists, physiologists, and neurologists as only a bio-physiological neurological organ phenomenon. For them, t*he human brain* is studied as completely *empty* of THD. Yet, biology, physiology, and neurology claim to be exact sciences while they entirely neglect to take into consideration the influence on the human brain of the strong presence of THD in it. Seen this way, these sciences can *hardly* be described as *exact sciences*.

As such, both social and natural sciences do not fulfill Ibn Khaldun's law of al-Mutabaqa (the good matching between the actual reality of things and what is said about them by humans). *Culture/the THD is the most central factor* in the making of human identity and the human mind which makes humans dominant social actors on earth as explained earlier.

This offers legitimacy to look *first* at the man as Homo-Culturus and not a Homo-Oeconomicus or a Homo-Sociologus or a Homo-Politicus. The Homo-Culturus underlines *the central fundamental nature of Man* while the other three Homos are deriving from the substance of the quality of Homo-Culturus, as underlined before. In other words, the Homo Culturus paradigm strikes at the very center of human nature, while the three other Homos paradigms make reference to peripheral dimensions of man's nature and activities. This view of man as a Homo Culturus sheds *new light* on the making of the human mind. Both THD and the mind are *unique distinct characteristics* of humans. The correlation between the two is found to *be a positive one on two levels*. On the one hand, it is inconceivable to think of the existence of the human mind without the intrinsic presence of THD in the human brain. It is assumed that other species do not have minds like the human mind because they do not possess the THD system gift. On the other hand, the great impact of THD on the making of the human mind is strongly displayed in the comparison between three types of the human mind: the illiterate mind, the educated mind, and the great-thinking mind.

The degree and the scope of access to THD wide knowledge make the differences between these human minds. The illiterate individual is rather poor in the THD doze: he/she does not read or write, and subsequently, he/she is deprived of knowledge and science in the largest and deepest sense of the word. As such, he/she is *handicapped* to have profound and wide thinking even on simple things and issues. In contrast, a person of great learned and thinking mind has good access to THD-wide knowledge. He/she has full skills in reading and writing and in the acquisition of wide and deep knowledge and science which permit him/her to be able to understand and explain better things and phenomena. All these features predispose him/her to contribute to the making of knowledge and science and perhaps introduce innovations in them as the example of Ibn Khaldun's praised mind has shown through his breakthrough of establishing a *New Social Science* in the fourteenth century called Ilmu al-Umrani al-Bashari *(the Science of Human Social Organization).*

Endnotes

1) The word 'knowledge' is used in this chapter to cover all branches of human knowledge, including what is called today scientific branches, like the Natural Sciences.

2) Published by Dar al Kitab Allubnani, Beirut (no date) pp.430. We will refer in short to this book by the term: *At-Ta'rif-* followed by A (Arabic) or F (French). The French version of this book is: *Ibn Khaldun, Le Voyage d'Occident et d'Orient,* AbdessalamCheddadi, Paris, Sindbad, 1980, pp.331. To my knowledge, *At-Ta'rif* has not yet been translated into English.

3) See my essay "An Appeal for the Indigenization of Arab Sociology into its Own Intellectual Islamic-Arabic Cultural Heritage" (in Arabic) *Alam Elfikr Journal*, Summer 2005.

References

Al-Jabri, M. A. (1988) *Formation of the Arab Mind I*(in Arabic), Beirut, Center for Arab Unity Studies.

Al-Jabri, M. A. (1982) *Al-Assabiyya and the State in Ibn Khaldun's Thought* (in Arabic), Beirut, Dar Attalia Publisher.

Al-Shaqaa, M. (1992) *The Islamic Bases in Ibn Khaldun's Thought and Theories* (in Arabic), Cairo, Al-Dar Al-Masriah Al-Lubnaniah.

Bothamley, J. (1993) *Dictionary of Theories*, London, Gale Research International Ltd.

Bucaille, M. (1976) *La Bible, Le Coran et la science*, Paris, Seghers.

Clayton, Ph., Simpson, Z. (2009) *The Oxford Handbook of Religion and Science,* Oxford, Oxford University Press.

Crane, D. (ed.1995) *The Sociology of Culture*, Oxford (UK) Blackwell. Compiègne, I. (2011) *La société numérique en question(s)*, Auxerre Cedex, Editions Sciences Humaines.

Cuche, D. (1996) *La notion de la ulture dans les ciences sociales*, Paris, La Decouverte.

Dahrendorf, R.(1974) *Homo Sociologicus*, Hamburg, Westdeutcher Verlag.

Dawood, N. J. editor (1974) *Ibn Khaldun, The Muqaddimah: an Introduction to History* (translated from Arabic by Franz Rosenthal, Princeton, Bolling Series, Princeton University Press.

Dhaouadi, M. (2003–2004) 'An Investigation into the Determinants of Ibn Khaldun's Umran Mind,'*Annals of The Arts and Social Sciences*, Monograph 208, 24.

Dhaouadi, M. (2001) 'The Legitimate Role of Ibn Khaldun's Personality Traits in the Birth of His Umran Thought'(in Arabic) *Journal of Al-Mustabal Al-Arabi*, no.265.

Dhaouadi, M. (1990) 'Ibn Khaldun: the Founding Father of Eastern Sociology,'*International Sociology*,**5**, no.3.

Dhaouadi, M. (1997) *New Explorations Into the Making of Ibn Khaldun's Umran Mind*, Kuala Lumpur, A. S. Noordeen.

Dhaouadi, M. (January 2008) 'Arab Cultural Concepts for Cultural Sociology,'*Contemporary Arab Affairs*, i,1, 76–82.

Dhaouadi, M. (2002) *Globalization of the Other Underdevelopment: Third World Cultural Identities*, s. Noordeen, Kuala Lumpur.

Discover Magazine, October 1996.

Dortier, J.-F. (2004) *Dictionnaire des sciences humaines*, Auxerelle Cedex, Editions Sciences Humaines.

Dortier, j.-F. (2005–2006) L'origine des cultures in *Les Grands Dossiers des Sciences Humaines*, no.1.

Encyclopedia of Sociology (1974) Guilford, Dushkin, Publishing Group, Inc.

Kraft, U. (2005) 'Unleashing Creativity,'*Scientific American Mind*, 16,2.
Kuper, a. (1999) Culture: *The Anthropologists' Account*, Cambridge, Mass, Harvard University Press.

Lacoste, Y. (1998) *Ibn Khaldu: Naissance de l'histoire, passé du tiers monde*, Paris, La Découverte/Poche.

Moore, K. (1982) *The Developing Human*, London, Saunders Co., 3rd Edition.

Morin, E. in *Science et Avenir* (Janv–Fév 2012, p.61).

Pedler, k. (1981) *Mind Over Matter*, London, Thames Methuen.

Robert, S. (1999) *Ibn Khaldun*, translated from Hungarian by Klara Pogatsa, AkadémiaKiado, Budapest.

Schmit, N. (1999) *Ibn Khaldun, Historian, Sociologist and Philosopher* (Arabic translation), Baghdad, Dar Al Maamoun.

Semashko, l. and others (2006) *International Sociology Review of Books*, **2**, 6, 829–38.

Shaw, S. J. and Polk, W. R. (1962) eds, Gibb H. A. *Studies on the Civilization of Islam*, London, Routledge and Kegan Paul.

Spillman, L. (ed.2007) *Cultural Sociology*, Oxford (UK) Blackwell Publishing.

Sternberg, R., (1999) *Handbook of Creativity*, Cambridge, Cambridge University Press.

Sternberg, R. (2003) *Wisdom, Intelligence, and Creativity Synthesized,* Cambridge, Cambridge University Press.
Toynbee, A. (1956) *The Study of History*, London, Oxford University Press. III.

Wallerstein, i. (2001) *Unthinking Social Sciences*, Philadelphia, Temple University Press.

Wallerstein, I. (1999) *The End of the World as We Know It,* Minneapolis, university of Minnesota Press.

Wieviork, M. (ed.2007) *Les sciences sociales en mutation*, Auxerre Cedex, Editions Sciences Humaines.

White, l. (1973) *The Concept of Culture*, Edina, MN, Alpha Editions.

Wilson, E. (1999) *Consilience:The Unity of Knowledge*, New York, Vintage Books.

Wolff, j. (September 1999) 'Cultural Studies and the Sociology of Culture,'*Contemporary Sociology,* 28, 5, 499–506.

Chapter III
Culture from a Different Outlook of Islamic Insights

Introduction

There are nowadays a number of reasons to encourage sociologists to study culture in order to seek a deeper understanding of the nature and manifestation of culture in the behaviors of individuals and societies. Globalization has become a hot topic for all at the beginning of the twenty-first century (al-Khülï 200: 515). In today's world, economic globalization is particularly prominent. But it is no exaggeration to say that most people on the five continents *feel that cultural globalization is even more present.* The information and communication revolutions naturally play a decisive role in the greater prevalence of communication, which serves to disseminate the hallmarks of cultural globalization to all corners of the globe, east, west, north, and south.

With regard to specialized branches of sociology, the study of culture is today one of the most prominent, leading to the emergence of this discipline of a field known as cultural studies, which focuses on the study of the cultural manifestation of human groups (During 1999:610; Long 1997: 529).

With regard to the cutting-edge fields in both psychology and sociology, we find, on the one hand, *cognitive psychology* (which is closely concerned with the individual above all as a cultural being) which is a pioneering branch of psychology (Martin and Rumelhart 1999:391); and, on the other hand, we find the branch of *cultural sociology* increasingly prominent among sociologists (Bonnel and Hunt 1999:350).

These factors alone confer legitimacy on efforts to devote greater attention to the study of culture and its contribution in order to highlight certain aspects that have been neglected by contemporary social science research. As we shall see, these are aspects of crucial importance for undertaking in-depth research on *the essence of culture*, which is the prime characteristic of the human race, and which has given it pre-eminence in the universe, as we have seen in the proceeding chapters.

Object and Purpose of This Chapter

The chapter is aimed at carrying out in-depth basic research on the essence and foundation of culture from *an Islamic epistemological viewpoint*, which differs from its equivalents in the contemporary social sciences. However, that cannot be accomplished without addressing the concept of culture in contemporary Western social science literature, which has been investigating culture and its manifestation since the nineteenth century, especially by means of anthropology and sociology.

Such a methodology will naturally prompt us to compare the concept of culture as seen from the Islamic epistemological viewpoint and from its Western equivalent. Comparative studies frequently shed fresh light on phenomena that may be difficult for the social sciences to understand and explain, and thus help scientific knowledge to move forward. This is *the primary goal* that the researcher seeks to attain. Our ambition here is above all to help to build a solid background for what has been called *Culturology* (White and Dillinghan 1973: 32–33) which, in our view requires a critical examination encompassing epistemology, theories, and concepts.

The Fogginess of Definitions of Culture in the Social Sciences

Anthropologists and sociologists have numerous definitions of the concept of culture. This suggests at least two things: either that culture is difficult to define, particularly when using the positivist criteria of sociology, or that culture is a phenomenon that is in itself complex.

We limit ourselves here to three definitions from anthropology and sociology. As mentioned before, the most famous definition of the concept of culture was given by the British anthropologist Edward B. Tylor in *Primitive Culture* (1871): "Culture, or civilization, taken in its broad, ethnographic sense, is that complex whole which includes knowledge, belief, art, morals, law, custom, and any other capabilities and habits acquired by man as a member of society" (quoted in *Encyclopedia of Sociology* 1974:.69).

The American anthropologist Leslie White connects the concept of culture among human beings to their ability to imbue things with meaning, which he calls *the ability to symbol*. This allows individuals to understand the meaning of things and also how they were created and how they are used (White and Dillingham 1973: 29). This ability in individuals is then defined as culture (White and Dillingham 1973: 9) and there is no individual without culture, and no culture without individuals (White and Dillingham 1973: 15–16).

According to the renowned anthropologist Alfred Kroeber, his American colleagues who studied culture and personality *failed to give a conclusive and clear definition of the nature of culture*. In his view, the debate on the matter remains open, despite the work of anthropologists such as Margaret Mead, Ruth Benedict, Edward Sapir, Ralph Linton, Abram Kardiner, and Franz Boas (Cuche 1996: 117). Furthermore, for some, the problem is not only the absence of a credible anthropological definition of culture but rather, *serious questions about the difficulty of studying culture* in the spirit of modern science and using its methodology. Radcliffe-Brown was of the view that culture does not have a material presence, but rather a very abstract presence. On that basis, others like him wonder *how there can be a science of something that cannot be seen* since there can be no science based on a reality that is neither perceptible nor visible (White and Dillingham 1973: 26).

For some anthropologists, the difficulty of studying culture goes beyond its definition to encompass other important aspects, such as: Does culture exist? Where is culture to be found? There have been various answers to these questions. Some authors have claimed that it is to be found in the behavior, and yet others say that culture is a manifestation that is a separate form of behavior, and *there are even those who deny the existence of culture altogether*. White holds that culture is located at three different levels: within humans, such as in their thoughts and feeling, in interpersonal behavior, and objects, in accordance with his concept that culture consists of objective and actual events that may be observed.

Sociologists, on the other hand, have *narrowed down* the scope of the term 'culture', which they take to mean what they call *the main ideas of society*. These include the beliefs, symbols, values, and customs of society. This standard sociological definition of culture is current, for instance, in most US sociology textbooks aimed at university students.

The foregoing brief survey of the concept of culture, in particular in modern anthropology, shows that *the notion of culture remains opaque* and is almost completely silent about what we wish here to call *the metaphysical aspects of cultural elements* (Dhaouadi 1997), or what we already have called cultural symbols/ THD: language, thought, belief, knowledge, values, cultural usages and myths. As outlined in this book, the THD is a synonym for the concept of culture widely used in modern social science. For us and most researchers in the social sciences cultural symbols/ THD represents *the main elements that distinguish the human race* from other living species as outlined recently in the Special Issue of the magazine of *Scientific American* (September 2018): "Humans: Why we're unlike any other species on the planet."

There is, for instance, an almost complete failure on the part of contemporary anthropologists and sociologists to address the metaphysical nature of the THD. Only with a small minority of scholars do we find rare and ambiguous terms suggesting that culture *is a super-organic human element*, as affirmed by the sociologist Herbert Spencer and by Kroeber (White and Dillingham 1973: 47), or that it is non-biological, as suggested by Tylor, or 'extrasomatic', following White or external and 'supra-biological', to use a term adopted by a number of sociologists.

These few *timid suggestions* that culture is a super-organic and super-biological element *remain ambiguous* with regard to the nature and essence of the THD that characterizes the human race. Things are not a little better when some anthropologists and sociologists see culture as an 'abstraction' (White and Dillingham, 1973: 24) or as something that 'has no ontological reality' (1973: 26). Given the general failure to clarify these terms, contemporary social science literature is devoid of epistemological theories of *the system of cultural symbols/ THD*. The tremendous intellectual fund of knowledge accumulated by the modern social sciences on culture remains content to describe cultural elements. Indeed, most anthropologists and sociologists agree that the word culture differs from the world of human biology, as suggested by the terms used above. Therefore, *culture*, as a contemporary Western concept widely used in the social sciences in particular, *is not dealt with* using the metaphysical point of view that we find in the Islamic approach.

In view of the neglect and absence of metaphysical touches in cultural symbols, contemporary social science is hardly objective, in the sense of a cognitive state that allows one to ascertain the truth as such quite independently of the mind of the researcher, unmarred by *prior* emotions, values, concepts or desires (Fay 2001: 202–220). The presence of metaphysical hallmarks, as will be shown, is an inherent truth that lies at the core of the THD. The various individual and social factors affecting the minds of Western researchers in the social sciences have prevented them from undertaking analysis and studies of culture from an epistemological viewpoint that gives full legitimacy to the presence of metaphysical touches. Thus, the tremendous body of knowledge accumulated by those sciences since the nineteenth century offers *a deficient reality* of the true specifications of cultural symbols.

Western social science ultimately *says more about itself* than it does about the inherent reality of culture.

The Concept of Culture from the Islamic Cognitive Viewpoint

When inquiring about the Islamic cognitive view of the THD or culture, the best way to determine their contours and meet the challenge of their essential nature is to refer to the Quran, the primary source of Islam at all levels. If our reading is successful in helping to understand the content of the Quranic verses pertaining to the THD, we shall have acquired the correct Islamic cognitive view of the nature of culture. And we shall thereby have armed ourselves with the most valuable Islamic concept of culture, which prompts the researcher to compare and possibly compete with the concept of culture as used hitherto and currently in contemporary social science.

Our methodology for revealing the THD and its nature in the Quranic text consists of three sets of questions:

1. Are there clear indications in the Quran that distinguish humans from other beings with regard to their capacity to act on behalf of God?
2. Are there Quranic verses that speak with complete frankness about the distinctiveness of the human race from all other living species?
3. To what do these Quranic verses attribute the distinctiveness and superiority of the human race?

Firstly, the Quranic text abounds in verses that accord a special, outstanding place to human beings among all other creatures, whether spiritual entities, such as angels, or animals that share the Earth with them. In other words, the image of the human in the Quran is of *a unique being*, who occupies first place in importance after God on this earth. Humans thus have no one who can contest their qualification to manage the affairs of this world and to assume the functions of sovereignty (vice-regency, stewardship) in it. We restrict ourselves here to five cases in which the Quran speaks with great clarity of the prominence of humans over other creatures. In Sûra/chapter *al-Baquara*(The cow 2:30), the Quran describes the human being Adam as the 'vice-regent of God on Earth: And then, your Lord said to the angels; I am placing *a vice-regent on Earth*'. There is little need to dwell on the importance of this office (the vice-regency of God on Earth) to which human beings were appointed to the exclusion of the angels and other creatures on Earth As to the absolute advantages of human beings described in three other verses of the same Sûra (chapter), *al-Baqara* (The cow) 2:31, 32,33) they consist of God bestowing upon Adam *more knowledge and learning* than on others, including the angels: "And He taught Adam all the names of beings, and then presented them to the angels and said: Tell me the names of these, if you be truthful" (al-Baqara) (The cow 2:31). As a result, God commanded the angels to bow down to Adam alone, as a third sign of honor and distinction to Adam: "And when we said to the angels: Bow down to Adam, they bowed down, except for Iblïs (Satan), who refused and became arrogant, and was among the disbelieves."

Al-Isrä Sûra (The night journey) 17:7 uses the verbs 'ennoble' and 'give preference' in order to demonstrate the two qualities of human beings as outstanding over other creatures on Earth: "We have ennobled the children of Adam and carried them by land and sea; We have provided them with good things, and given them clear preference over many of the beings that We have created."

These Quranic verses clarify beyond the shadow of a doubt that *humans are special beings* who are outstanding and superior to other creatures of the Earth and to angels. The Quranic view of the human race thus represents a complete cognitive (epistemological) break with the theory of evolution of Darwin and his associates, because the creation of Adam, in the Quranic view, represents *a special case of creation* which is quite separate both from the angels and from the realms of other creatures here on Earth. The creation of human beings stands apart from all other instances of creation by the gift of knowledge and learning that God granted to humans alone. It is because of this *strong cognitive* ability that it was legitimate to make Adam the vice-regent of God by ennobling him and giving him preference on Earth, and having the angels bow down to him.

Two verses from the Quran council the angels' bowing down to Adam to God's blowing of his spirit into him: "And when I have fashioned him and have *breathed of my spirit into him*, fall down in prostration to him"*al-Hijr* (The rocky place) 15:29, *Sad* (The letter Sad) 38:72.

It is fully legitimate to query the meaning of the words 'my spirit' contained in these two Sûras because the way the verse is structured suggests that the injunction to the angels to bow down to Adam follows the breathing of God's spirit into him. In other words, there is a strong, if not causal, connection between the act of breathing the divine spirit into Adam and God's exhortation to the angels to bow down to him. As is well known, the word 'spirit' in the Quran has various meanings, first and foremost that of infusing creatures with life. *The Tafsir* exegesis *of the two Jalals* states: "Attaching the spirit to him constitutes an ennoblement (an honoring) of Adam. The spirit is a genial body by means of which human beings live, thanks to its influence in them" (al-Mahalli and s-Suyuti, 1993: 457). The celebrated modern Syrian Quranic exegesis 'Afif Abdulqadir al-Fattah Tabbara' provides the following exegetic explanation of the words 'my spirit' in the verse: "I breathed into him of my power, in other words, when I infused him with spirit whereby, he might live, that spirit being of my own doing…fall down to him in prostration" (Tabbara, n. D.).

We conclude with the exegesis of Sheikh Mutawalli ash-Sha'rawi, the most famous Egyptian exegetists in the modern age. He explains the meaning of 'the spirit of God' and its being breathed into Adam as follows: The breathing of the spirit of God does not mean that the breathing was done to infuse life by blowing into Adam's mouth. Rather, this represents the diffusion of the spirit to all parts of the body.

Scholars have differed over the definition of the spirit. For my part, I think that it is safer not to go too deeply into that matter because the Truth Almighty is He who says: "And they ask you about the spirit, say: The spirit is from the command of my Lord; the knowledge you have been granted is but little" *Al-Isra* (The Night Journey) 17:85 (ash-Sha'rawi, nd, vol.12: 694).

It is clear from the content of this exegesis that the meaning of the words 'my spirit' is quite simply the power of God to infuse Adam with life, of whose secrets human beings have no knowledge, which is why Sheikh ash-Sha'rawi advised against going too deeply into that matter.

Sticking to this explanation of the meaning of the words 'my spirit' does not allow Adam the human being to occupy the office of the vice-regent of God on Earth and of the angels to bow down to him in honor of his special and outstanding nature. God infused not only human beings with life but also all living creatures. Hence the mere infusion of human beings with life does not qualify them alone to act as the vice-regents of God on Earth. There is therefore a need to seek *some other meaning of the words 'my spirit'* which might strongly suggest the distinctive and superior position of human beings over other creatures by virtue of their stewardship of Earth as the vice-regents of God.

This is where, in our view, *the role of the social sciences* in helping Quranic exegesis comes in to guide them to the appropriate meaning to be given to the words 'my spirit' in the verses "And when I have fashioned him and have breathed of my spirit into him, fall down in prostration to him"*al-Hijr* (The rocky place) 15:29 Sad (The Letter Sad) 38:72. Many contemporary exegetists draw on the discoveries of modern science in explaining numerous Quranic verses concerning the creation of human beings and understanding the functioning of the human brain and body, and especially the relationship of human beings to natural phenomena in the universe, such as the sun, the moon, stars, mountains, seas, volcanoes, and earthquakes, all of which have served to reinforce the idea of the inimitability *(I'jaz)* of the Quran. There are increasing numbers of publications, symposia, and conferences in this field in the modern Islamic world. We agree in this respect with Dr. Zaghlul an-Najjar, who stresses that it is not possible to understand many Quranic verses without relying on highly credible scientific discoveries concerning human beings and the natural phenomena of the universe.

In the same way and to the same extent, modern exegetists are also called upon to make use of the fund of contemporary social science learning concerning the understanding of the behavior of individuals and communities, and the dynamism of societies and human cultural hallmarks. These disciplines certainly help to get closer to the meaning of the words 'my spirit' in the verses referred to above. The disciplines of anthropology, sociology, and psychology all agree that human beings are distinct from other beings by virtue of what those disciplines call *culture* or what we have termed the THD: language, thought, knowledge and learning, religion and cultural values and customs, which, from the perspective defended here, qualified humanity in the past, and continue to do so in the present and future, to play the role of vice-regent of God on Earth. In other words, the phrase "I have breathed of my spirit" means that the divine breathing into Adam is first and foremost *a cultural breathing* in the contemporary sense given by the social sciences to the term culture. The breathing of cultural symbols/the THD into Adam alone conferred upon him, to the exclusion of others, the function of the stewardship of Earth, and the attendant bowing down of the angels to him. Such a cultural reading of the words 'my spirit' in these verses makes clear just how much-*enhanced credibility* the explanation of Quranic verses has if exegetists draw on modern scientific knowledge.

The Cognitive Quranic Foundational View of Culture

It is clear from the foregoing that *the Quran has a cognitive (epistemological) view concerning the THD as a distinctive feature of the human race*. The divine cultural breathing into Adam, to the exclusion of others, is thus a breathing that has, according to the Quranic view, *metaphysical roots and a metaphysical nature.* Its source is not the world of Earth, but rather the world of the heavens, of which the creatures of Earth were deprived, and which was given to human beings alone. The Quran speaks with complete frankness of the metaphysical nature of the cultural breathing for which human beings alone were singled out: "And when I have fashioned him and have breathed of my spirit into him, fall down in prostration to him." In other words, *the cultural breath* deep within Adam *comes from the divine essence itself.* There is thus no room in the Quranic vision for doubt about the essential metaphysical nature of the THD that distinguishes the human race from other living species.

On the other hand, as noted, most social science and Western sociological literature is almost completely silent about the metaphysical aspects of culture. It studies and analysis the cultures of societies using a descriptive or positivist method without bothering to raise cognitive (epistemological) questions about the nature of culture as a unique hallmark of individual humans and of human societies, shying away from examining the features of things that are not subject to the world of sensory perception or quantity. It is an objective, scientific failing to reject the metaphysical despite its strong presence at the heart of the THD, one that restricts understanding of the behavior of individuals and the dynamism of societies and civilizations. How can one have confidence in the findings of social science research, which studies culture *stripped*—for reasons of epistemology— of its essential metaphysical hallmarks? Hence, the Western social sciences should not merely study the religious factors involved in understanding the behavior of individuals and the dynamics of societies (Heath, 2000), but also draw on the cognitive (epistemological) vision of religions as a source of scientific understanding (Ebaugh, 2002), as this chapter endeavors to highlight with respect to culture.

Cultural symbols/ THD have *a transcendental or metaphysical character* that makes them different from the components of the human body and the material world. Individuals thus have a tri-dimensional identity: a system of the THD, on the one hand, and body and soul, on the other hand. It is the THD that is the most prominent and decisive in the determination of the identity of individuals, and hence their behavior. As referred to earlier, the five most important transcendental/ metaphysical traits are as follows:

1. Cultural symbols/ THD do not have *weight or volume*, unlike the biological and physiological components of living creatures and the material world.

2. As a direct consequence, cultural symbols enjoy *ease and rapidity of transmission* over time and space.

3. Cultural symbols are undiminished by sharing, unlike elements of the material world. If we give others something from our knowledge, learning thoughts, creeds, cultural values, language, and so on we lose nothing.

4. Cultural symbols have a great capacity to survive for long periods of time in human societies. Indeed, through written language, their longevity may even be indefinite. The thoughts of Socrates, Aristotle, Ibn Rushd (Averroes), al-Ghazali, Ibn Khaldun, Rousseau, Descartes, Hume, and other thinkers and scholars would not have survived or enjoyed such a long period of survival if it had not been recorded in the letters and words of the varied languages that enable it to meet the challenge of immortality. Languages have a particularly prominent role to play with regard to the preservation and immortalization of the collective heritage of human communities. Written languages, especially, enable human communities to record, *preserve and immortalize their collective memory* despite the extinction of those communities' organic and biological presence as living organisms; despite their changes of place and the fact that successive generations of their members live in different ages from their own. The complete preservation of the language of the Thad (a letter/sound thought to be unique to Arabic) in the

Quranic text is a prime example of the capacity of the language of the immortal text to safeguard the collective memory and heritage from the oblivion that is brought about by the passage of time, changes in the environment, and the temporary nature of corporeal organic biological existence.

These transcendental/metaphysical dimensions are not limited to written language alone. The oral use of language is also coupled with transcendental and metaphysical meanings. Humankind's encounter with the metaphysical dimension in its various manifestations thus becomes inevitable: individuals see it in their dreams, it fills their imagination and they encounter it at close quarters in their religious experiences.

5. Cultural symbols possess an extraordinary power to imbue individuals and societies with enormous energy, enabling those who possess it to triumph over the greatest challenges, in all their many forms. By way of example, the values of freedom, justice, and equality have been shown, over the long course of human history, to be cultural symbols capable of endowing individuals and communities with colossal, surging energy similar, to some extent, to overwhelming metaphysical forces which no one can withstand. Such is what the words of the Tunisian Arab poet, Abu l-Qasim ash-Shabi, suggest: "If, one day the people choose life, fate must inevitably respond." The source of peoples' real volition lies in the world of the THD. That is, when people unite to defend freedom, equality, justice, and other human values, and their right to independence and self-respect, their reaction becomes like the reaction of fate, "which neither preserves anything nor leaves anything behind." This explains why people resort to talking of miracles in respect of certain individual or collective events, which enter the historical record despite the lack of concrete evidence for them. They are manifestations of the decisive impact of cultural symbols in giving birth and

momentum to people's behavior in human societies and civilizations throughout the ages.

The metaphysical roots of human cultural symbols possessed in the Quranic view need to be made more concrete in the world of human and social reality so that they may be used in current field research in the social sciences. The transformation of the abstract notion of the metaphysics of cultural symbols/the THD to a down-to-earth formulation of the manifestations of their metaphysical features provides a procedural concept that social science researchers may use at the core of their fieldwork and theoretical research. This procedural concept contributes to beginning the reconciliation of all non-objective factors influencing the behavior of the individual and society, which the positivist view, in particular, *avoids taking into account* in understanding and explaining collective and individual phenomena. The remainder of this chapter deals with some of the implications of this perspective.

The Features of Some of the Transcendental Aspects of the THD

It is not sufficient here to affirm that cultural symbols/ THD are a central part of the breathing of the divine cultural spirit into human beings. We need to clarify how the breathing or insufflation of the divine cultural spirit manifests itself in certain cultural symbols. We shall present here *three* examples of cultural symbols that reflect some features of aspects of the insufflation of the divine cultural spirit.

Language and Its Metaphysical Traits

The Quran affirms the eternal nature of the divine essence. "He is the First and the Last" (*al-Hadid* (The iron) 57:3). "Everyone on Earth must pass away; there shall remain but the face of your Lord, full of glory and munificence" *(ar-Rahman* (The merciful) 55:26–27). Several cultural symbols are also described as being long-lasting or even eternal.

Building on the points made in the previous section, let us briefly consider language as the most important of all cultural symbols which *immortalize* the life of individuals and human societies.

It is not difficult to establish the features of metaphysical touches in linguistic structures, for *language is the Mother of all cultural symbols* (White 1959). As such, language is better suited than other elements to carry flashes of the Islamic cognitive view of the world of human cultural symbols. It is possible to confine ourselves to mentioning and defining four features with respect to the identification of the metaphysical features of language as *a capital element* of the making of the THD by which the human race is distinguished.

1. The place occupied by language in the information revolution, which Toffler and other experts in this field speak about, is well known. The speed of instant communication carried out in the twinkling of an eye between individuals and societies today is achieved basically by means of the primary unit, which is the linguistic structure as represented by the word (such as the noun, adjective, verb, particle, number, and symbol). The speed of transmission of the written and spoken word in today's world is not only attributable to modern communication technologies but is also profoundly influenced by *the nature of language itself*, as humankind's most important cultural symbol. Communication by means of language, in both written and spoken form, has radically transformed our world, and improved communication technologies such as telephone, fax, and the Internet, Facebook, have endowed it with the qualities to wonder and marvel. Human communication and instant news gathering have, despite the enormous distances, become imbued with what we might term the metaphysical dimension of human existence in this world, from which a new expression of the THD identity of human existence takes shape.

The conventional formulation of the nature of human beings consists in their having a body and a soul. Under the new conception of human existence, crystallized by the information revolution, human beings are bodies, either reposing on the earth's surface or floating in space, but interconnected and present there by means of language at incredible distances either on Earth or in the vastness of space. This new type of duality casts the old metaphysical aspect of human identity (the spirit) in a new guise which, despite its novelty, continues to have strong links to the world of the metaphysical and the untangible, which human beings have been unable, in general, throughout their long history, to eliminate entirely from their perception, intuition, and intellectual and scientific thinking (Hunt 1982:.315–353).

2. Field data confirm the power of language *to immortalize individuals and groups* symbolically, across time and space. At the collective level, written language in particular enables human groups to record, preserve, and immortalize their collective memory, despite the evanescence of their organic and biological existences as groups and despite the possibility of subsequent generations changing their location and mode of life in later times. It is the same with individuals, great writers in particular (Parsons 1966). In short, our linguistic structure permits the stock of a people's memory and the ideas of outstanding individuals to enjoy a greater or lesser degree of the features of *immortality and the eternal.*

3. The capacity of cultural symbols to enable individuals to enjoy a kind of immortality has improved thanks to successive technological discoveries in the field of advanced electronics. The recording of sound and color images by the process of digitization is a lively example of the ability of cultural symbols to immortalize the words, sounds, and live, natural images of living beings and inanimate phenomena.

4. At the cultural level, the use of language is also coupled with metaphysical meanings. Do individuals of all creeds and religions not use the spoken word in their existential reflections, their supplications and entreaties to their God, or to whatever else they believe to be eternal or holy? Set apart from other living beings by language, human beings are able to liberate themselves from the physical constraints of this world and establish relations and links with the metaphysical world. Through its linguistic ability, humankind succeeds in disengaging from worldly and momentary concerns.

Metaphysical Aspects of the Values of Freedom, Justice, and Equality

How is it that individual behavior, in certain particular cases, is transformed into behavior that appears to have been influenced by metaphysical forces? To clarify this fully, it is necessary to make several preliminary basic remarks.

Field observation both of the world of human beings and of the worlds of all the other animal communities shows, on the one hand, that the behavior of the latter is profoundly affected by *instinct,* and that, on the other hand, human behavior is primarily influenced by *cultural symbols/ THD.* This explains the complete, or nearly complete, congruence in the behavior of each species of animal, insect, bird, and reptile over successive generations and over time and space. As regards the human race, there is *considerable diversity* in the patterns of both the principal and marginal types of behavior from one civilization to another, from one society to another, and from one generation to another.

Contemporary sociologists and anthropologists agree that such differences in patterns of behavior among and within human societies are basically attributable to the influence of the world of cultural symbols/the THD (culture) upon them, in the form of religions, traditions, customs, cultural values and cognitive systems (Smelser and

Smelser 1967: 80–87). In other words, human beings, unlike animals, derive freedom of action, freedom of choice, and freedom to differ from others in the world of cultural symbols. Traces of the Islamic metaphysical, and epistemological aspects are strongly present in this interpretation. The divine essence, in the Islamic cognitive view, has absolute freedom, volition, and choice—it acts as it wishes. Thus the phrase, "I have breathed of my spirit into him," in the Quranic verse must imply the attributes of choice, freedom, and volition-naturally within the relative limits of humankind, as is the case, according to the Islamic view, in respect of the field of human knowledge ('the knowledge you have been granted is but little'). It is not surprising, then, that specialists in human behavior fail, in many cases, to provide accurate predictions of it.

Psychologists and sociologists often base their predictions of human behavior on *a rigidly deterministic foundation of rules* that do not acknowledge the principles of freedom, volition, and choice when weighing up the factors influencing human behavior. This stems from *a false epistemological view* that causes them to fail to distinguish between the effects of cultural symbols and instinctual, material factors on the behavior of members of the human race. Specifically, such an approach does not acknowledge the existence of the metaphysical element, as suggested in this chapter, at the core of the THD/cultural symbols.

In this regard, it is striking that cultural values such as freedom and justice, proclaimed by human beings throughout their long history, *have received no attention worth mentioning* from modern scholars of individual and group behavior. Despite the key role played by these cultural values in driving individual and group behavior in ancient and modern times, social scientists, in general, have refrained, and continue to refrain from recognizing their roots and the profound significance of their influence on human behavior. It seems to them that these *are metaphysical things*, the study of which is the preserve *of philosophers, not scientists*. This is a further example of the epistemological deficiency from which contemporary positivist science suffers by its aversion to seeking reconciliation between the perceptible world and the metaphysical world, whatever the nature of the latter may be (Philips 1985). Human beings' unique enjoyment of freedom and the capacity for choice is a characteristic linking individuals to the world of metaphysics. In most religions and beliefs, the deity is distinguished by this quality. Human beings are thus unique in partaking of this quality, relatively speaking, with the deity. The Quranic text refers specifically to the metaphysical link, which is the source of individuals' freedom, volition, and the capacity for choice, all of which stem from 'And when I have fashioned him and have breathed of my spirit into him' *al-Hijr* (The rocky place) 15:29). In the Quranic perspective, conditions were thereby brought together within this rational being (by giving human beings a share of freedom, volition, and choice) for him to be the sole candidate for the vice-regency of God by means of the fund of cultural symbols. Specifically, "We offered the trust (of responsibility, freedom of choice) to the heavens and the Earth and the mountains, but they declined to bear it and were afraid of it. But man assumed it. He has proved a tyrant and a fool." *al-Ahzab* (The Confederates 33:72).

Cultural Symbols That Imbue Human Beings with Great Energy

Therefore, neither the world of animals and beasts nor the world of machines and devices endowed with modern artificial intelligence enjoys the quantity and quality of the nature of the world of cultural symbols/ THD possessed by human beings.

A representative example, perhaps, of the metaphysical dimensions of the world of values as cultural symbols is the al-Aqsa intifada waged since 28 September 2000 by the Palestinian Arab people against Israeli occupation and settlement in order to liberate their land to achieve justice and equality.

Faced with overwhelming Israeli superiority in military equipment *the Palestinians have adopted new methods of resistance.* The al-Aqsa intifada is, like its predecessor in 1989, called the 'revolution of the stones', because it is with pebbles and stones that Palestinian children and youths face heavily armed Israeli occupation army. The second innovative strategy consists of young Palestinians turning themselves into *human bombs* against the Israeli military and the civilian population inside Israel itself. Finally, the Palestinians also fight on Israeli-occupied land with conventional weapons, resisting settlers and the occupation forces with weapons and materials that are limited in comparison with the lethal modern weaponry possessed by the opposing forces.

The pressing cognitive question that must be asked is: what are the decisive factors that have resulted in the phenomena of the Intifada, its means of resistance, and its continuation for inconsiderable period of time, despite the fact that the Israeli State has assassinated the leaders of the Palestinian resistance, committed numerous massacres in the towns and villages of Palestine and sought to destroy the main stays of the infrastructure of Palestinian society? There is little doubt that resistance with pebbles and stones against an army equipped with tanks and lethal modern weaponry is military and physically unrealistic. The matter is much worse with regard to those Palestinians who have chosen certain death by turning themselves into human bombs against the occupation. The motives and driving forces for such Palestinian behavior in combat are certainly not material. They are, rather, *high moral forces* rooted in the system of Palestinian cultural symbols/the THD.

Human beings are by nature the bearers of cultural symbols. This is what explains the logic of individual behavior and collective actions, which have a proven ability to defy overwhelming physical facts, as we have seen from the example of the Palestinian intifada. The resistance of Third-World liberation movements in the last century is further testimony to the credibility of the capacity of the THD to create, drive and orient individual and collective human behavior toward goals that, materially, seem extremely difficult or impossible to achieve. The imprisonment of many Third-World leaders in the modern era did not prevent them from fighting to withstand the vastly more powerful material forces of the colonizer. There is no more credible explanation for their final victory over the occupiers than the factor of their being armed with moral weapons or the weapons of the world of cultural symbols, in accordance with our concept of the THD in this chapter and the book at large. Popular uprisings against oppressors in ancient and modern times merely demonstrate the importance of the ammunition that human beings may derive from the world of cultural symbols, which transform those individuals' energy into a challenge to the greatest military force the tyrant or colonizer may possess.

The Lack of Weight and Volume of Cultural Symbols

The ease of transmission and spread of cultural symbols throughout the world is due to their lack of certain perceptible material elements, as indicated before. The physical weight and volume of objects represent the basic perceptible elements of the world of substance, and in the final analysis, it requires human effort to convey physical objects from one place to another. While cultural symbols/ THD themselves are by their very nature devoid of weight and volume, the artifacts in which they are embodied may well be material. Thus, cultural symbols have volume and weight when printed on paper. The transport of large numbers of encyclopedias, books, documents, magazines, and newspapers across a distance needs considerable time and effort if the distance is great and the means of transport primitive. Modern means of transport have facilitated the transport of the heaviest objects from one place to another, but volume and weight remain two decisive factors in relation to the swift conveyance of things and the physical effort needed to transport them. Nonetheless, cultural symbols can in principle be disembodied, as they are by modern technologies.

The view that cultural symbols possess features that make them similar, to a large extent, to metaphysical entities closely corresponds with the Quranic vision of the nature of cultural symbols. The mixing of clay with the divine cultural spiritual breath in the creation of Adam gave him a tri-dimensional nature: body, THD, and spirit/soul. Cultural symbols are, therefore, pregnant with metaphysical transcendental elements in the tri-dimensional make-up of the nature of human beings. *This view of the THD represents the core of the Islamic view of culture.* This is the principal and legitimate *paradigm* in which the sociology of culture should be rooted in the Arab and Islamic world.

Toward Sociology of the Metaphysics of Cultural Symbols

It is clear from the preceding pages of this chapter that we are in the process of establishing what we might call the *sociology of the metaphysics of cultural symbols* on an Islamic epistemological foundation. We have derived the metaphysics of cultural symbols, on the one hand, from methodological analysis of the nature of cultural symbols themselves, and on the other hand, by employing the Islamic epistemology of cultural symbols. As such, our vision in this chapter represents a theoretical framework with cultural foundations and an Islamic epistemology. It is thus a perspective *that differs completely from the positivist one.* This new view of cultural symbols responds strongly to the growing calls from sociologists to integrate and draw on religion to understand and explain the phenomena under study and establish theoretical thinking at the heart of these sciences (Ebaugh, 2002).

The careful study of the essence of cultural symbols must be included in the category of *basic scientific research.* Cultural symbols, as we have seen, represent the essence of human beings. There is, therefore, little doubt that uncovering their nature and secrets is *a priority,* as a deep understanding of cultural symbols is conducive to helping us better to understand individual behavior and the dynamics of human society.

Our choice of the Islamic cultural perspective for studying the metaphysical features of the system of cultural values stems, on the one hand, from the lack of interest and failure of the positivist and other perspectives to investigate this topic, as we have shown in this chapter. On the other hand, our approach is at the cutting edge, concretizing the embedding of religious thought at the heart of the social sciences. In our view, what is important for the advancement of science is not stubborn adherence to a particular perspective and methodology, but using the appropriate perspective and methodology to understand and explain the phenomenon under consideration. There is, then, strong legitimacy for adopting the Islamic cultural perspective as an *alternative* to the conventional positivist perspective, the principles of which were established in the nineteenth century, and which, in the view of many sociologists today, are *no longer adequate*. These scholars believe that the time has come for three fundamental changes at the heart of sociology.

Sociologists need to be convinced that there is no single scientific methodology for research in the social sciences. There is a call today to *legitimate diversity* among the scientific methods that sociologists may employ to study phenomena of interest to them (Risman and Tomaskovic-Devey 1998).

This new approach among sociologists holds that sociology is able to adopt and employ a range of intellectual and theoretical frameworks without thereby prejudicing its central vision (Risman and Tomaskovic-Devey 1998:10). Our perspective thus remains faithful, in respect of its object of study, to the core of sociology. This part of the chapter focuses its analysis on the system of cultural symbols that have always had priority in sociological and anthropological studies. What makes this chapter particularly faithful to sociology and anthropology is its attempt to *impart a new scientific character to* the understanding of the system of cultural symbols/ THD through its focus on their metaphysics, derived from the cognitive view and the metaphysical observations of Islam. Discovering the metaphysical manifestation in the system of cultural symbols justifies what *was missing* at the core of the cognitive stock of modern sociology and anthropology, and our understanding is thereby completed of the most important traits that distinguish the members of the human race from other species.

This new generation of sociologists believes that sociology is a science that is characterized epistemologically by creativity and innovation which qualifies it to be at the cutting edge in proposing new ways of conducting scientific activity. What is important in this regard is not the adoption of a particular method of scientific research, but rather the use of a methodology that is actually capable of building a solid scientific structure. This must first of all be capable of identifying the social and cultural factors that underlie the genesis of the phenomenon under consideration since the explanation of phenomena by means of social and cultural influences is incorporated into the heart of the sociological perspective. This is what distinguishes the sociological perspective from both the psychological and the biological perspectives in their explanation of human behavior. Whatever research methodology we choose must have as its ultimate goal the discovery of the cause or causes that have contributed and are contributing to the formation and genesis of the phenomenon. However, the search for the causal factors of social phenomena *should not be limited to the quantitative factors* stressed by positivism since the nineteenth century. Rather, the search for the causes of social phenomena must also aspire to identify qualitative causes, which positivism has not sought to use.

Comparing it with the perspective of Western sociology, our perspective in this chapter could be placed under the heading of what the American sociologist Randall Collins (1982) has called '*non-obvious sociology*', which uncovers hidden processes behind the obvious. It is a discipline that demonstrates that obvious matters *are not necessarily* the most significant.

Our use of the Islamic cultural perspective, based upon the metaphysical epistemology of cultural symbols, is *a new type of paradigm* for social scientific research. What we have endeavored to do in this chapter is to define a new method for scientific work on what is hidden from the gaze of most contemporary sociologists and anthropologists in their studies of culture. It gives sociology a touch of creativity, allowing it, as a science, to be innovative in its capacity to define new methods of scientific research. Our approach in this chapter and in the entire book is *to move from* what we previously have called *Exclusive sociology to Inclusive sociology.*

The Harmonization of Our Perspective with Reflexive Sociology

There is little doubt that the Islamic cultural perspective proposed here for the study of culture is one that brings together a number of cognitive viewpoints constituted essentially by sociology, philosophy, and religion. This is a formula that is rejected by conventional positivist science but is accepted and welcomed by the new trend at the heart of sociology (Bunge 1999; Risman and Tomaskovic-Devery 1998). Furthermore, the sociology called for by Pierre Bourdieu supports, to a large extent, our approach in this chapter. Bourdieu's cognitive intellectual project, termed 'reflexive (self-critical) sociology' (Bourdieu and Wacquant 1992:.43–70), has little respect for the boundaries drawn between cognitive specializations (Bourdieu and Wacquant 1992:13). Hence, this sociology calls for new methods to be devised that are conducive to understanding and explaining social phenomena with a high degree of credibility. It thus represents a challenge to the current divisions and patterns of thought that are prevalent in the social sciences. Bourdieu urges the adoption and use of multiple methodologies in the study of social phenomena and the research carried out by sociologists (Bourdieu and Wacquant 1992:32). He believes that sociology, as a cognitive view, needs to be a total science or Inclusive sociology in our terms (Bourdieu and Wacquant 1992:.30). In the words of Marcel Mauss, sociology must provide us with *the total social fact* capable of restoring the basic unity of scientific research, which has long been torn apart by the boundaries between cognitive specializations, empirical fields, and techniques of observation and analysis. On this basis, Bourdieu is vehemently opposed to separating methodological fieldwork from theory in sociology, defining *méthodologisme* as the tendency of the research to separate the intellectual effort required to devise methodologies from their profitable use in scientific work itself. Bourdieu believes that mastery of research techniques often results in poverty of sociological theorizing regarding the phenomenon under consideration. True sociology, then, is that which always preserves the strong link between method and thought (Bourdieu and Wacquant 1992:.31–32).

Bourdieu concludes from his defense of reflexive, self-critical sociology that such an approach is not the enemy of the modern scientific view, but that it does go against numerous positivist conceptions of the social sciences, and also against the absolute separation introduced by the positivist social sciences between the quantitative and qualitative aspects of the phenomena studied (Bourdieu and Wacquant1992:.39). It is thus evident that this model of sociology urges a linkage and dialogue between both sides of the duality, in respect of both the phenomenon studied and sociological practice. The latter must, on the one hand, give priority to the study of both the qualitative and the quantitative aspects of the social phenomenon, and on the other hand, open a dialogue between fieldwork and theoretical work to address the challenge of understanding and explaining social phenomena and processes.

From the above, it may be said that our Islamic cultural perspective on the study of culture falls within the kind of sociology called for by Bourdieu and others including mine represented by Inclusive sociology (Bourdieu and Wacquant1992:43–70). We sharply criticize contemporary Western sociology (Exclusive sociology), which almost completely ignores the metaphysical features of cultural symbols/the THD, some of which we have mentioned in this chapter and others. Instead, we today call upon Muslim sociologists to desist from merely imitating their Western counterparts, both past and present, with respect to epistemology, methodology, and theory.

Western sociology today suffers from a crisis of epistemological unity, which (Wallerstein 1999:1–16) has urged all sociologists to overcome. Sociologists in the Islamic world are fully qualified to respond to this pressing call and implement it in Islamic sociological thought in the twenty-first century. The perspective of Islamic culture is at the cutting edge in his field: the unity of all knowledge and sciences. Consequently, there is *no place* in this culture for the phenomenon of two cultures and antipathy and hostility between cognitive and scientific specializations. In other words, Islamic sociology, based on the power of the absolute, unifying epistemology of human knowledge, is well placed to be wholly impervious to the epistemological crisis that Western sociology and other types of knowledge and science are experiencing today.

The study of the THD from the Islamic cultural perspective is entirely legitimate in relation to Islamic sociology, as this chapter makes clear. On the one hand, it will contribute to rooting this discipline in the perspective and epistemology of the mother culture of Islamic societies, and on the other hand, the metaphysical features of cultural symbols will help to open new, previously unclear, cognitive horizons in the legacy of contemporary sociological thought on culture—that enormous, complex whole, in the words of Tylor.

The Arab Nation and Its Cultural Cohesiveness and Solidarity

Our concept of the THD/cultural symbols allows Arab sociologists to talk, for example, about the societies of the Arab world as region whose near and distant parts are united by the principal Arab-Islamic cultural symbols: Islam and the Arabic language, and *the culture resulting from both*. As such, the Arab nation is, first and foremost, a product of those cultural symbols, which transcend the factors of geographical proximity, economic exchange, and military alliance between Arab countries. The spontaneous Arab and Islamic consciousness and solidarity among the masses and the elite in the societies of the Arab world are attributable, in our view, to what might be called, in the words of Ibn Khaldun, *cultural group solidarity*. The author of the *Muqaddima* believes that the bond of kinship is the most important basis for solidarity and unity ('asabiya) among individuals:

"(Respect for) blood ties is something natural among men, with the rarest exceptions. It leads to affections for one's relations and blood relatives, (the feeling that) no harm ought to befall them nor any destruction come upon them. One feels shame when one's relatives are treated unjustly or attacked, and one wishes to intervene between them and whatever peril or destruction threatens them. This is a natural urge in man, for as long as there have been human beings." (Ibn Khaldun, 1993: 102; 1967, Vol. I:264).

Thus, Ibn Khaldun's conception of 'asabiya as solidarity toward those of blood kinship is a phenomenon with bio-genetic roots. But by cultural solidarity, we mean that the sharing by individuals, groups, and communities of similar and homogeneous cultural symbols (language, beliefs, ideas, cultural values, norms, and customs) automatically inclines them toward rapprochement and solidarity with one another and makes them passionate supporters and defenders of all those who share those cultural symbols. Arabs and Arab Muslims use the words *'brothers and sisters'* when they speak about other Arab and Arab Muslim countries and their citizens. Obviously, *the shared THD* is behind their feeling of brotherhood and sisterhood toward each other.

What distinguishes cultural solidarity from kinship solidarity is that the former is much more open-hearted and humane than the latter in terms of its capacity to embrace an enormous number of humanity's millions, possibly extending to include all of humankind, from all races, nations, ethnic groups, tribes, and clans. The sharing of a single set of cultural symbols by the races of humankind creates, by means of something like a magic hand or what we have called the cultural symbolic soul (Dhaouadi, 1992) a bond of brotherhood, sisterhood, and solidarity between individuals, nations and groups that do not know one another and may be separated by hundreds and thousands of miles.

Conversely, the sweeping, spontaneous, Arab-Islamic sense of solidarity between the men and women of the societies of the great Arab world cannot be explained by Ibn Khaldun's narrow concept of kinship solidarity.

It may thus be said that the sense of solidarity between Arab societies, which share key cultural symbols, is *an established, objective* fact, as long as the Arab peoples maintain their affiliation to homogeneous cultural symbols, at the forefront of which are the Islamic religion and the Arabic language, together with the culture of both. This sense may be now weakened, now strengthened under the pressure of various factors, *but it is never extinguished*: its nature is eternal as the Arab-Islamic cultural symbols among the peoples of the Arab world.

In its weakest state, this sense of solidarity is a latent, silent force in the depths of the collective Arab-Islamic subconscious. In full bloom and vigor, the sense of solidarity among the Arab peoples becomes a raging, roaring force akin to the defiant metaphysical forces in the world of the collective Arab-Islamic consciousness against the enemies of the Arab and Islamic world. There is little doubt that the manifestations of the strong and quasi-eternal bonds between the Arab peoples find a sound explanation in our cognitive Islamic view of the nature of cultural symbols.

Talk of the issue of Arab unity past and present acquires powerful legitimacy from the strong cultural unity that binds together the societies of the Arab region. The fact that most of these people speak Arabic and profess the Islamic faith constitutes a foundation that is unequaled in strength, solidity, and continuity over time by any economic, military, or political union of peoples. *Language and religion are thus two key elements* of what we have termed the THD (language, thought, knowledge/science, beliefs, cultural values and customs, and myths): All are elements that, on the one hand, have the capacity for longevity across time and space, and may even be eternal. On the other hand, the observation of authoritative social scientists suggests that when individuals, groups, and peoples share a common language, faith, and culture, this strengthens the bonds of interrelation, affinity, and solidarity more than any other factor. Accordingly, it may be said that *the propensity of European societies to enjoy long-term unity is weaker than that of Arab societies*. The countries of the European Union, for example, speak a variety of languages while Arabic is the common language spoken by Arab societies. We are here in the presence of two different types of unity between peoples.

The European Union represents an attempt to unite its members, particularly at the economic, political, and legal levels. It is a unity that strives to serve pressing momentary interests that ensure the course of progress in those societies. The unification of language and religion among these countries is not an issue that is included in the plan for European unity at the present time. Indeed, the constitution of the European Union respects linguistic and religious diversity. Given the absence of linguistic unity and the weak level of the Christian faith (owing to the multiplicity of sects and churches), the European Union that is coming into being is *only a circumstantial and temporary union*, in whose long-term continuity there can be no confidence as the example of the United Kingdom shows. Only complete unification with respect to the key cultural symbols (the big markers of language and religion) qualifies peoples for long-term and possibly eternal unification at the level of cultural unity.

The countries of the Arab region between the Gulf and the Atlantic Ocean, while lacking many elements of economic, political, and legal unity, are, on the other hand, superior to the societies of the European Union at the level of cultural unity, as most of the inhabitants of the Arab world speak Arabic and profess Islam. Hence, the project of Arab unity finds powerful legitimacy in the consciousness of affinity, solidarity, and unity among the Arab peoples, thanks to the shared cultural background that has existed between them for many centuries. The fact of cultural unity between the Arab peoples is thus *prior* to and independent of factors of geographical, economic, military, and political unity and the variables of time and place. As seen with regard to the strong ties of cultural unity between the Arab peoples (cultural *'asabiya*), the reader of this chapter will probably not be surprised if we conclude by affirming that the superiority of cultural symbols over other factors that unite societies and peoples—in terms of the longevity and strength of unity—finds strong legitimacy in our thesis of cultural symbols from an Islamic cognitive perspective, which gives a prominent place to the metaphysical.

It thus appears that, on the one hand, the application of our concept of cultural symbols/ THD in order to understand and explain the foundations of the enduring solidarity of the Arab nation over the ages, and, on the other hand, our in-depth analysis of the nature of culture in the rest of this study, are capable not only of contributing to a renewal of the horizons of Arab-Islamic sociological and anthropological thought (see-al Ansari 2001) but also of going beyond that to become highly legitimate candidates for influencing the perspectives of modern western sociological and anthropological thought concerned with the study and theory of culture.

Note

1. The words supra-biological, super-organic, and supra-organic are used by Western anthropologists and sociologists to describe the cultural aspect of individuals, although in their analysis these scholars do not refer unambiguously to culture as having metaphysical features, as we demonstrate in this chapter.

References

Al-Ansari, M. J. (2001) 'Mas Uliya min… tajdid al-fikr al-arabi…? (Responsability for… the renewal of Arab thought …?'*Al-Bahrain ath-thaqafiya* (Cultural Bahrain), Damascus: Dar al-Fajr al-Islami, 30:140–144.

Al-Khuli, Usama, A. (2000) *Al-arabwa-I – aulama (The Arabs and globalization),* 3eme edn., Beirut: Markaz dirasat al-wahdaal-arabiya.

Al Mahalli Jalal Ad-Din Ibn A. and S. Suyuti, Jalal Ad-Din (1993) 'Abdurahman Ibn Abi,'*Tafsir al-Jalalain (The exegesis of the two Jalals),*7, Beirut: Dar Ibn Khatir.

Ash-Sha'Rawi, Shaikh Mutawalli, n. D. Tasfir ash-Shaikh Mutawalli (Exegesis of Shaikh Mutawalli).
Bonnel, V., and Hunt, L. (1999) (eds)*Beyond the Cultural Turn,* Berkely, CA: University of California Press.

Bourdieu, P., and Wacquant, L. J. D. (1992) *Réponses. Paris. Editions du Seuil.* (Transl. 1992 as An introduction to Reflexive Sociology) Chicago, IL: University of Chicago Press).

Bunge, M. (1999) *The Sociology-Philosophy Connection,* Piscataway, NJ: Transaction.

Collins, R. (1982) *Sociological Insight: An Introduction to Non-Obvious Sociology,* Oxford: Oxford University Press.

Cuche, C. (1996) *La notion de culture dans les sciences sociales.* Paris: la Découverte.

Dhaouadi, M. (1992) 'The cultural symbolic soul: An Islamically inspired research concept for the behavioral and social sciences,'*American Journal of Islamic Social Sciences,* 9 (2), 153–72.

Dhaouadi, M. (1997) 'Fi-d-dalalat al-mitafiziqiya li-r-rumizath-thaqafiya (On the metaphysical meanings of cultural symbols),'*Alam al-fikr (The World of Thought),* 25 (3), 43–49.

During, S. (1999) (ed.) *The Cultural Studies Reader*, 2nd edn., London: Routledge.

Ebaugh, H. R. (2002) 'Return of the sacred: Reintegrating religion in the social sciences,' *Social Sciences Journal for the Scientific Study of Religion*, 21 (3), 385–395.

Encyclopedia of Sociology (1974) Guilford, CT: Dushkin Publishing Group.

Fay, B. (2001) *Contemporary Philosophy of Social Sciences*. Oxford: Blackwell.

Heath, M. (2000) *Religion and New Immigration. Center for Religion and Civic Culture*, Los Angeles, CA: University of California Press.

Hunt, M. (1982) *The Universe Within*, New York: Simon and Schuster.

Ibn Khaldun (1993). T*he Muqaddima, Beirut: Dar al-Kutub al-ilmiya*, (Trans. In 1967 as The Muqaddimah: an introduction to history) Princeton, NJ: Princeton University Press.

Long, E. (1997) *From Sociology to Cultural Studies*, Oxford: Blackwell.

Martin, B. and Rumelhard, D. (1999) (eds) *Cognitive Science*. 2nd edn., San Diego, CA: Academic Press.

Parsons, T. (1966) *Societies: Evolutionary and Comparative Perspectives*, Englewood Cliffs, NJ: Prentice Hall.

Philips, D. C. (1985) *Philosophy, Science, and Social Inquiry*, New York: New York Press.

Risman, B. J. and Tomaskovic-Devey, D. (1998) (eds) 'A window on the discipline, symposium,'*Contemporary Sociology*, 27 (1), 1–28.

Smelser, N., and Smelser, W. (1967) *Personality and Social Systems,* New York: John Wiley and Sons.

Tabbara, Afif Abdulqadir *al-Fattah*, d. *Tafsir, juzya sin* (Exegesis, Part ya sin (sura 36)), vol.23, Beirut: Dar al-Malayin.
Wallerstein, I. (1999) 'The heritage of sociology, the promise of social science,'*Current Sociology*, 47 (1), 1–37.
White, L. (1959) *The Evolution of Culture*, New York: McGraw Hill.

White, L., and Dillingham, A. (1973) *The Concept of Culture,* Edina, MI: Burgess International Group.

Chapter IV
Are Cultural Symbols Behind Human Long Lifespan?

Introduction

In this chapter, as in the others, we use the Third Human Dimension (THD) as an interdisciplinary concept. In it, we practically leave no stone unturned in searching for the reasons behind the link between the THD and the human longer life. The THD refers to those traits that distinguish *radically* the human species from the rest of the other living species: Written and spoken language, thought, religion, knowledge/science, laws, myths cultural values, and norms...are specific human characteristics. As we said, we call them the THD because humans are usually seen as having a bi-dimensional identity (body and soul). On our part, we consider the human identity as made of *three components (body, soul, and the THD)*. So, the THD is part of the human identity. With them only has come the very legitimacy of the domination of the human race over the other species. As such, the THD constitutes the most fundamental distinct basis of the human identity. The impact of THD on humans ought to be remarkable and broadly extensive. That is, their influence on humans is assumed to *be wide-ranging*. They affect various dimensions of the human social actors. I argue in this chapter that the THD has bearings not only on the social, cultural, and psychological aspects of humans but also *on their biology*. This justifies my claim that humans are first of all cultural-symbolic beings before being social. Looking at the THD this way and shedding insights into the credibility of those assumptions will make the THD set an acceptable interdisciplinary concept. In this chapter, I limit my use of the THD mainly to the disciplines of biology, social sciences, and human sciences, especially religion and philosophy.

The THD is Central to Human Identity

The main idea I am proposing here is the following: "Man is by nature a THD being," before being social by nature. As mentioned before, this claim is based on a number of observations regarding five features that strongly distinguish humans, from the other species:

1. The process of the human body's (bio-physiological make-up) growth and maturation is very slow compared with those of other living beings.
2. In general, humans have a longer lifespan than those of most of the other species.
3. Humans are radically distinguished from the other species by their dominant and powerful role in the running of the planet earth and beyond.
4. Humans are decisively privileged from the other living species by the THD system…
5. The human identity is made up of three parts: the body, the soul, and the THD. It is fully *a tri-dimensional identity*.

Then, the legitimate question that ought to be raised now is the following: Are there relationships between those five human distinct features? There is certainly a direct relationship between 1and 2. Because the slow human body growth and maturation require necessarily a longer lifespan to enable the full realization of the different and diverse phases of bio-physiological growth and maturation. Consequently, the link between 1 and 2 is of causal nature. Unfortunately, neither Scientific American(SA) magazine nor that of the New Scientist have provided me with hard scientific data that explain the slowness of the human body's growth and maturation. SA has simply advised me (October 19, 2005) to do the following: "You might try searching anthropology websites for possible answers." My analysis of the issue in question adopts indeed *an interdisciplinary social sciences perspective*. As to the human tri-dimensional identity, it is also a direct outcome of the human organic body, the soul, and the THD.

The search for a relationship between man's domination factor and his remaining four distinct features strongly shows that features 1 and 2 hardly predispose man to be the unique dominant being over the other species. Since humans are, for instance, much weaker physically than many other species. As such, it could implicitly be hypothesized and suggested that Man's dominant role is strongly related to features 3 and 4, already underlined: The human dualistic identity and the THD.

The THD's principal role in the determination of human destiny goes even further than just the central place that man occupies in the world/the universe. The importance of the THD manifests itself indirectly in features 1 and 2. The slow human body growth and maturation could hypothetically be explained by the fact that human global growth and maturation involve *two fronts*: The bio-physiological front as well as that of the THD.

In contrast, the body growth and maturation of the rest of the species are overall of rapid nature, because it is assumed that it is due to the absence of the THD in the non-human species. In short, while the growth and maturation of non-human species is *uni-dimensional: bio-physiological* dimension, their human counterparts are bi-dimensional. That is, human growth and maturation involve two fronts: the cultural-symbolic dimension as well as the bio-physiological dimension. So the rapidity or the slowness of the entire growth and maturation processes of the species depends on the variable/factor of the uni-dimensionality (the bio-physiological) or the bi-dimensionality (the bio-physiological and the THD) of the entities of living species. The following table shows the THD centrality in the human entity. This loudly supports the strong legitimacy of my idea which advocates that "man is by nature a culturo-symbolic being." In brief, my hypothesis here shows it does not explain only the impact of CS on human slow body growth but also *the CS/ THD impact on human lifespan*, the domination of the world/universe by humans, and humans having dual identities.

The Table

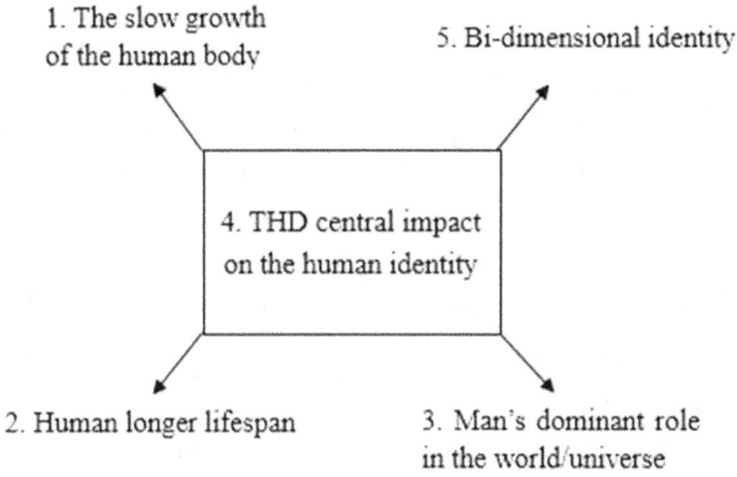

THD centrality in the human identity as shown above leads to the emergence of my new concept which I would like to call Culturobiology as manifested in 1 and 2 in the table. That is, the THD slows the bio-physiological pace of the processes of human growth and maturation and consequently the very human genetic design. For instance, the human bio-physiological longer lifespan is considered to be a necessary condition that meets the much longer time, in terms of years and decades, that the THD needs to be grown and fully matured. It is well established by observation and especially in cognitive psychology that THD is slower in their growth and maturation than their bio-physiological counterparts in humans. We are told by specialists that humans reach their peak bio-physiological growth and maturation around the age of 25 years (Rischer, Easton 1992:423). As to human thinking, acquisition of knowledge/science, and religious experience—as essential components of the THD—they cannot reach their peak stage of growth and maturation at the age of 25. But they rather reach their ultimate growth and maturation after the age of 40 years. In other words, these very important elements of the THD need much longer human lifespans to be well-developed, grown, and matured. So comes the necessity for humans to have a special genetic-bio-physiological design to meet the human THD's requirement for a longer lifespan in order to be able to develop, grow, and reach their peak maturation among humans.

The thesis of my concept of culturobiology is quite different from that of sociobiology. While the latter considers biology as the basis for many human social behaviors, culturobiology sees that the already made suitable human genetic-bio-physiological design or a longer human lifespan is the outcome and response to the longer time it takes the THD to be fully developed, grown, and matured. This new outlook of the THD/culture shows that the latter has a global influence on humans: their behaviors and their genetic-bio-physiological entity. This is in contrast to the common traditional view of contemporary anthropology and sociology which mainly restrict culture's impact on people's behaviors and societies' social structures. This means that THD has a global impact on humans: their bio-genetic-physiological design, their individual behaviors, and their societies' dynamics. The table above clearly shows that THD is too central to human nature. This hard fact justifies our claim that the THD has indeed a *global effect on human destiny and affairs*. That is, humans are fundamentally cultural-symbolic beings. As such, the THD is the first direct and indirect strategic key that social scientists have at their disposal to understand and explain human behavior both in its individualistic and collective sense.

The THD and Its Crucial Use in Soft and Hard Sciences

Our main thesis in this chapter would like to strongly argue that the study of the behaviors of human individuals and the dynamics of their societies must give priority to what distinguishes them most from other living non-human beings and their collectivities. We consider the THD (language, religion, knowledge/science, thought, laws, myths, cultural values, and norms…) as *the crucial divide* between the human species and the rest of the other species. The meaning of THD corresponds more and less to that of the term culture as used by contemporary social sciences. In our view, THD constitutes the most central and fundamental part of individual and collective identities. In other words, THD is the very core of the human species, as argued in this book. On one hand, other known living non-human species could compete neither quantitatively nor qualitatively with the human species on the THD scale. In short, the THD is the privilege of the humans and their communities. On the other hand, without the THD, the homo sapiens cannot alone claim leadership and domination in this world/universe. As such, *the THD is second to none* in the determination of the human's supremacy over the other species. So, they are indeed the ultimate center of humans as a distinguished special species.

The first-class centrality of the THD in the making of human individuals and communities makes its impact on human affairs very compelling, including *human biology*. That is, we can hardly imagine the human social action of social actors and their collectivities without the THD input. At one level, the THD is often the direct micro and macro-motivating force of social action in social life. At another level, the THD plays a screening role for both inside the social actor's personality and the outside environment's potential influential factors to which human communities and their members are exposed. In other words, the THD represents a sort of *filter* to the influential forces that orient and ultimately shape human social action. They are, so to speak, *the checking board* that determines the particular kind of social action which individuals and collectivities find themselves engaged in. Our assumptions on the nature of the THD (their first-class position in the identity-making of humans and their communities and their weightful impact on human social action) lead us, consequently, to take *a critical stand* to those social science analytical perspectives that give priority to the economic-socio-structural and biological (sociobiology) factors as capital determining forces of social action. In their explanations of individual behaviors and societies' dynamics, Marxists emphasize the determining role of economic factors, functionalist sociologists stress the socio-structures of collectivities and sociobiologists give great importance to biological parameters.

While social scientists must give credit to all these factors in their analysis of individual as well as collective behaviors, *they must not,* however, conceive the impact of the bio-economic-socio-structural variables as automatic unilinear irresistible forces like the impact of instinctive drives on behaviors among animals. There is overwhelming evidence from contemporary social sciences that the differences in behaviors among individuals within the same community or belonging to various societies are largely due to cultural differences. That is, human behavior is strongly culturally determined. This is not true only of biological factors but also of their socio-structure-economic counterparts. The impact of the latter on the individual behaviors and their collectivities are systematically *cross-checked* through their own cultural systems which often play the role of a vigilant referee. As such, in the final analysis, the impact of CS/ THD on human social action is very compelling indeed. With this extreme importance in mind, it must become the first reference framework of social scientists for both comprehension and explanation of human behavior and the community's dynamics.

The current strong emergence of both cognitive psychology (1) as the leading subdivision in the field of psychology and of cultural sociology (2) as also a front-line growing sub-discipline of sociology is a strong indicator that the role of the THD in the analysis of society's dynamics and the individuals' behaviors is increasingly getting widely recognized in the social sciences. This change of perspective is quite legitimate because of the central role the THD plays in the making of human affairs. Thus, it is hardly an exaggeration to expect other branches of social sciences and biology-related sciences to give more attention to the impact of the crucial parameters of the THD in their attempts to comprehend and explain *the human bio-genetic design* and the behaviors of human agencies as well as the dynamics of human collectivities. The rather imposing impact of the THD on the orientation as well as the ultimate determination of human social action, is not only limited to its comprehension and explanation both in the micro and macro senses.

Our conceptualization of the THD constitutes also an interdisciplinary conceptual framework. That is, an intellectual vision of the human world where the THD is considered the most central component of the total human identity. With these semi-paradigmatic uses, the THD could become a strong potential social science framework for *social theory building* about the behaviors of social actors and the collective social action of human communities as well as of the human bio-genetic make-up. As defined, a social theory is an intellectual perspective that can explain aspects/phenomena of social life. In other words, the THD could empower social science researchers to actively engage in theory building at the micro and macro levels of human social life. Since humans and their collectivities are perceived here as profoundly culturally oriented by nature. There is hardly any surprise to consider the THD as a general resourceful kit for wide legitimate and credible theory building about human societies and their members.

As such, we consider the THD another disciplinary masterpiece concept for the social and human sciences. But its great importance is hardly limited to these soft sciences. We have found also that hard/natural sciences could benefit considerably from our concept of the THD in their understanding and explanation of biological phenomena. The latter is the focus of this chapter. We use the concept of the THD to examine *a very unusual biological case study that has not been known to have been addressed and analyzed both by hard sciences as well as by soft sciences*. As an interdisciplinary concept, the THD is used to help explain their determining impact on the longer human lifespan.

The Phenomenon under Study and Its Methodology

The phenomenon studied in this chapter and its thesis is inspired neither by our readings in the social sciences and other related disciplines in English, French, and Arabic nor by our academic and scholarly contacts with colleagues in universities, research centers, intellectual seminars, and conferences.

We were shocked when the idea of the correlation between THD and longer human lifespan began in 1995 to assert gradually itself in our thinking. We asked ourselves: How come we have not seen any reference to this correlation in all the written materials we have come across in social sciences and in other disciplines? We had a strange feeling. But our discomfort was lessened somewhat when we started to tell colleagues and students about that correlation. Practically, all of them have also expressed their *dismay and amazement* that they themselves have never thought of this relationship between THD and the longer lifespan of members of the human species.

As such, one can hardly hope to find help in modern literature in the different fields of science on this subject matter. We even had difficulty having easy access to information about the average lifespan of the members of other living species. Such information is certainly important for the investigation of the relationship between THD and the lifespan of living species. We decided to write to the National Geographic Society as well as to *Discover* Magazine in the USA asking them if they have ever published studies, articles, and books on the longevity of animals. We received no answer from *Discover* Magazine. But, the National Geographic Society wrote back to us (Feb. 23, 1995) saying, "We have not published an article on the longevity of animals nor was I able to find a book on the subject in our library. However, I did find the enclosed chart in the World Almanac and Books of Facts 1994 that might be of some help." It is against this background that we were led to take *two contradictory positions*: (1) we thought that our idea about the correlation between THD and longer human lifespan was completely an ill-founded idea. This is why there has been no known mention of it or (2) we thought that *the idea* of this correlation is really *a new one*. So it deserves to be explored in order to evaluate its credibility. W*e chose option (2)* in spite of the enormous scientific challenges and risks involved for *the lonely researcher.*

Common people's observations as well as those of scientists concur that members of the human species live, on average, *longer lives* than the members of most other living species. It is, therefore, legitimate to ask why there is this difference. We attempt to answer this question through basic facts and observations from *two perspectives.* The first perspective relies heavily on modern bio-genetic science. As to the second perspective, it draws its explanation from the THD framework and religion and philosophy. As mentioned, the THD is language, knowledge, science, thought, religions, cultural norms and values, and other the THD by which the human species is greatly distinguished from the rest of other species. But, how legitimate to make a hypothesis that links human longer lifespan to THD? Such a hypothesis appears to be a sound one. On the one hand, humans live longer than most other species. On the other hand, they are alone privileged with the THD. So the link between human longer lifespan and THD could be potentially a strong one, as it will be shown below. A good hypothesis has great potential to lead to credible science if it passes the rigorous cross-checking test of its claims.

The Human Species' Longer Lifespan

We need here to take a look at the very recent average age differences between the members of the human species, and those of a limited sample of animals. The average lifespan in years of certain animals are as follows: lions (15), tigers (16), sheep (12), cows (15), pigs (10), rabbits (5), gorilla (20), horses (20), elephants (40)(4). But the average lifespan of humans is significantly longer than the average lifespan of the animals referred to here. Even before the modern medical scientific revolution, the average human lifespan in many human societies was around 35 years or more.

The Bio-Genetic Perspective on the Human Lifespan

Modern bio-genetic science is inclined to explain the longer human lifespan by the bio-genetic factor in the human species make-up. Scientific research continues to underline the crucial importance which the genes play in numerous aspects of human identity and behavior. In the last decades, some scientists have even explained the social behavior of humans through facts and information gathered by the science of biology and genetics. The new sub-discipline of sociobiology is the outcome of that process. Sociobiologists explain a number of human social behaviors like suicide and forbidden marriage between sisters and brothers by the deterministic logic of human biology and genes.

Geneticists, likewise, view that the individual's lifespan is strongly determined by the kind of genes he/she has. On the one hand, they consider that the age of 120 years is somewhat the maximum age human beings could reach. In other words, the inherent make-up of genes of the members of the human species allows them to reach the age of120 years. In contrast to this, the genes of non-human species don't permit their members to reach that very long age. It is, therefore, the type of genes that each living species has that ultimately determines the maximum number of years in which certain members of a given species could live. Modern scientific evidence strongly shows that the human type of genes plays a crucial role in the making of a longer human lifespan. Much was written in magazines and newspapers about the world's oldest French lady: Jeanne Calment who was 120 years old (6). The former French president, François Miitterand, had given her a diploma for being the oldest known human individual in the world. Scientists have found out that reaching very old age appears to run into families. Mrs Calment's mother died at the age of 86 years while her father lived longer than her mother. He died when he was 93 years old (7). Thus, it is through the working of the genes that old age could become a hereditary phenomenon among humans.

Scientists believe that individuals who live very long may have a type of gene that has a special resistance against the harmful impact of the chemical remains that result from the nutrition process in the human body. These chemical residues are assumed to damage more seriously the DNA of the majority of the population as it grows older (8). This scientific observation implies that the human species may have a better immune system than the other living species in dealing with the chemical remains mentioned before. However, this observation may offer just an apparent explanation of what may make humans enjoy longer lifespans. In order for such an explanation to have stronger credibility, it needs to explain why the better immune system of the genes has largely been confined to the human species. We don't know at this time if the sciences of biology and genetics have their own scientific explanation for this human peculiarity. I e-mailed in early 2004 the *Scientific American* (SA) magazine asking for this information: Why do human bio-physiological development and maturation take much longer time than their counterparts in the non-human species? SA has not sent me any reply. The latter should be helpful in shedding light on the reasons behind the human's longer lifespan.

The Need for a Complex Thinking Approach

Even if these two sciences have a solid bio-genetic explanation for that, this should not discourage scientists and researchers outside of the sciences of genetics and biology to look for other potential or even crucial determinant factors that could also be involved in the making of the longer human lifespan in question. This is quite legitimate in a time when scientists and researchers are more and more convinced of *the complex nature of the factors* which may co-influence particularly a given human phenomenon. The French sociologist and philosopher,

Edgar Morin, speaks of the necessity of the adoption today by modern scientists, researchers, and scholars of what he calls *the complex thinking approach* (9). In other words, scholars, scientists, and researchers should avoid the use of a strict simple reductionist approach in their study particularly of human phenomena which are complex by their own nature. Our interdisciplinary concept of the THD in this chapter is in line with Morin's perspective.

On the one hand, to explain the distinct human longer lifespan solely by bio-genetic factors is a very *reductionist approach*. It can hardly see, beyond its frontiers, any plausible influential other factor(s) that should seriously be taken into consideration in the understanding and the explanation of the human longer lifespan. On the other hand, our search for the causes behind the phenomenon of the human longer lifespan has shown us that *there are more factors involved* in the latter than the mere narrow territory of the bio-genetics of humans. As pointed out earlier, we use the THD perspective in order to help understand and explain the cause(s) behind the longer lifespan that the members of the human species are privileged to have. We have already stressed that there is a strong reason for our choice of the THD interdisciplinary concept. The THD is what distinguishes humans most from the rest of the living species. It is through the ability to use the THD that the human species has acquired *its uniqueness.* As such, the THD becomes the most important variable to take seriously into account in our analysis of multiple human phenomena including the biological ones. Based on the great importance of the role of the THD to the unique destiny of humankind, we could restate our former hypothesis: on the one side, humans are absolutely unique because of their enormous skills in the use of the THD. On the other side, they are also considerably unique in their relatively longer lifespan. Is there a link between *these two unique human characteristics?* And what kind of relationship is there between them? Let us take a look, through some illustrative examples, at how the presence of THD in humans would necessarily require a longer lifespan for them. In modern social science terminology, there appears to be a strong correlation between these two human characteristics.

The Pace of Growth and Maturation of the THD

As mentioned before, the human species is distinguished by its possession and use of the complex system of the THD. The latter needs a long time to grow, evolve, and reach their maximum maturation. While the growth and maturity of the human body reach their peak around the age of 25 or before, while the beginning, for instance, of the development of mature complex thinking hardly appears before the human individual is 20 years old. But an adequate mature thought does not often materialize before the person is around forty years. And the peak maturation of human thought usually crystallizes by the age of forty and beyond (10). All this shows that the growth, evolution, and the reaching of final maturation in human thought and other THD-related dimensions require indeed longer lifespans for humans. In other words, the development and the full maturation of the world of THD need roughly *more than twice* the years needed for the growth and the complete maturation of the human organic body.

This state of the THD's slow growth and maturation appears to be the outcome of an initial slow innate nature of the human brain growth and development parts relevant for the full use of the complex world of the THD. It has to do here with a sort of innate bio-genetic-neuro make-up design of the human brain that needs a longer time to use and develop fully the entire spectrum of human activities associated with and elaborated by the THD.

Years Difference Between the Child's Muscular and Linguistic Development

In order to be more specific on the gap in years between these two realms of human development, we compare here the child's body pace of growth with that of his/her linguistic development in order to underline the slower development of the THD. At the age of five months, the child can roll over his/her body at all sides. When he/she reaches eight months, he/she can sit alone, and at eleven months, he/she can sit alone, and at his/her first birthday, the child is able to walk alone (11).

As to the development of the child's language, it goes through several phases. Observations show that the child begins the process of vocalization and cooing between four and eight weeks of age whether he/she is alone or with others. Between 12 and 16 months, the child's first words appear as imitations of an adult speaking, usually nouns with emotional significance 'Mama', 'Daddy'. At the age of two years, the child has a good understanding of language and he/she can in general make two and three-word phrases. Between four and five years of age, the child uses more adult like grammar with some complex *constructions still missing.* His/her vocabulary at this age is between 5,000 and 7,000 words. He/she masters the grammar language around the age of 12 years (12).

These two examples show that the development and maturation of *the child's language*—the most important component of the THD— *needs a much longer time than the growth and the maturation of his/her body* which permits him/her to stand and walk alone at a very early age. The human being's possession of the THD and its implications on the behavior of the human species lead inevitably to the discussion of the brain/the mind because the latter is the place per excellence for the development and maturation of the THD.

The Brain/Mind and the Human Longer Lifespan

In order to explain this discrepancy in the pace of growth and maturation between these two realms of the human entity, we can refer to what may be called an objective descriptive approach which is widely used by modern science in order to understand and explain phenomena. Scientists are of the view that the members of the human species need longer lifespans because of their brain/mind (where is the THD). The explanation of this relationship has been described as follows:

1. Observations show that the growth and maturation of the organs of the human body take a much longer time (in years) than the growth and maturation of the organs of the bodies of other living species. Scientists have explained this difference by the presence of the brain/mind in the human species. Because of this *slowness* in the pace of growth and maturation of the organs of the human body, the individual members of the human species will, therefore, require longer lifespans, so the organs of their bodies can reach their peak of growth and maturation. What is at stake here is *the human biology* itself. Its processes of growth and maturation are greatly delayed when compared with those of non-human biology. There is a fundamental question that has to be raised here. It is a basic research question: What does the human brain/mind (the THD) have to do to be able to slow down the biological processes of the human body? Unfortunately, most biologists have confined themselves to the description of the workings of human biology. Consequently, the issues that may be involved in these matters—and they are beyond the frontiers of human biology—have hardly been raised.

2. Man's brain/mind has made what sociologists call *socialization* (basically, through the THD) *a very long process* in terms of the number of years needed for its accomplishment when compared with the length of the process of socialization among the rest of other living species. Human socialization consists of the individual's learning the THD of his/her milieu/society such as language, religious beliefs, customs, cultural values and norms, and the heritage of knowledge/science. With successful socialization, the individual becomes a full member of his/her milieu/society. In other words, complete and successful socialization makes the individual assimilate entirely into the melting pot of their own society. This can hardly be achieved within a very short time. But rather, it could last until the age of adolescence. The lengthy period of human socialization is due

largely to the slowness, difficulty, and *the complexity* of mastering and assimilating the THD of society into the basic personality of the individuals. Human socialization is a continuing process and it has practically no end, particularly in ever-changing modern societies. But again, there is a need to go beyond the simple sociological description of the process of socialization. We need to ask: What is in the THD that makes them not easy to learn and master quicker and at an earlier age? In other words, what is special about them that make them slower than the biological processes in their growth and maturation? Is there *any hidden dimension* in them that both modern natural and social sciences have not dealt with?

Cultural Determinism and the Human Lifespan

On the one hand, as it has just been shown, the longer lifespan of members of the human species is to be accounted for, in great part, by the factor of the THD underlined in this book. There is some sort of *cultural determinism* behind the average longer lifespan of the members of the human species. On the other hand, living species that don't have THD don't need as a matter of fact longer lifespans; because their biological and physical growth are determined in shorter periods. So that each species could fulfill its functions at the appropriate age and subsequently guarantee the continuity of its offspring inspite of its very short lifespan. But the distinction of the human species by the THD has made the human species' longer lifespan *necessary* for its own survival. This has been achieved in two ways:

(a) As pointed out earlier, the presence of the brain/ mind in the human species *delays* by many years the achievement of full growth and development of the human organic body. While the maturity of the body and organs of certain animals can be attained at the age of one or two years, the maturation of the body and organs of humans can hardly be fully realized before the age of fifteen years. This bio-physiological fact requires that *humans must live longer in order to fulfill their full bio-physiological growth and maturation* and be able to secure the continuing existence of the human species through the reproductive process.

(b) As underlined before, the nature of the growth and maturation of THD is much slower than that of the growth and maturation of the human body. In order for the THD to perform their full and complex functions and roles in the individual's life and the development of human societies and civilizations, it becomes compelling that the members of the human species have longer lifespans. The time factor in years and decades is *so crucial* for the THD's full development. In other words, the full-blown maturity of the THD is not only space (social milieu) dependent, but it is also strongly *time dependent*. It becomes, therefore, a compelling necessity for humans to enjoy longer lifespans. In modern social science terms, there is a strong correlation between the presence of THD and the need for a longer lifespan (13).

It is evident from the analysis presented here, that the longer human lifespan is largely a response to the needs of the THD. In other words, it could be said that those needs of the THD *have dictated,* so to speak, a special bio-chemico-genetico-neurological structure of the human species designed in order to permit the members of the human species to enjoy a longer lifespan than the other living species which are deprived of the THD. Our perspective is somewhat opposite to that of *sociobiology* which claims that numerous human social behaviors are triggered by the genes and the biology of the human body.

Our view here shows rather that it is the cultural factors which have in turn influenced the very action of the biology and genes of the human species. It has to do here of what we may call *acculturized biology*. That makes our THD concept visibly interdisciplinary. That is, it could be used to explain the socio-cultural as well as the biological dimensions of the human entity. The thesis developed here is quite compatible with the new emerging scientific outlook which calls upon scientists, scholars, and researchers to expand their visions beyond the narrow views through which they look at and explain complex phenomena. They need rather to adopt multi-dimensional views. The latter study phenomena as complex entities that are, at one level, influenced by different factors and, on another level, the influential factors are influencing and influenced agents at the same time (14).

Biology, Genetics, and the THD

The strong correlation established so far between the longer human lifespan and THD is hardly mentioned in the enormous corpus of modern science in general. As pointed out before, both genetics and biology make no reference to the role of THD in the length of the human lifespan. For these two branches of exact sciences, the question of the longer human lifespan has to be analyzed and explained *only in genetic and biological terms*. This does not mean, however, that biologists and geneticists don't make any mention of THD. On the contrary, some even speak of the THD as what makes humans human (15). Nevertheless, they neither look at human biology and genetics through those humanizing THD as we have done in our concept of acculturized biology, nor do they say very much about the relationship between the THD and human biology and genetics let alone the very nature of the THD as well as why they grow and mature slowly. In other words, there is hardly any real help we could seek from these two branches of modern science in order to answer some of *the Basic Research questions* on the essential nature of the THD. Unfortunately, as already mentioned, my Spring 2004 e-mail contact inquiry from *Scientific American* on this subject has been met with total silence.

Modern Social Sciences and the Missing Transcendence

When we examine the profile of modern Western social sciences, we hardly find reference to the concept of *the transcendence* of the THD as used here. For us, THD transcendence is displayed in the following four features: (1) The THD is volumeless and weightless. (2) The THD has a potential long/eternal lifespan. (3) The THD has a potential rapid/instant mobility through space and time. (4) The THD charges humans with fantastic motivation and energy that makes them so powerful and defying like metaphysical forces.

As part of the notion of culture, as defined by the British anthropologist Edward B Tylor, the THD has received special attention, particularly from the disciplines of anthropology and sociology. Both have extensively studied religion, language, cultural values and norms, magic, science, thought, myths, etc. Countless anthropological and sociological studies have been written about the functions, the pace of change, the diffusion, etc. of the THD in human societies. Contemporary anthropologists and sociologists have widely used the concept of Culture/ THD in order to analyze and explain individual and collective social behaviors in human societies. For instance, common cultural values and religious beliefs in societies are used to account for the patterned collective social behaviors of individuals of different systems of personalities. Common THD is, thus, *a fundamental basis* for social solidarity and, subsequently, for the emergence of the phenomena of human societies themselves. As such, the concept of the THD is crucially important in the study of the dynamics of human behaviors be that of the individual or the collectivity. In contrast to non-human behavior which is basically determined by biological instincts, most human individual and collective social behaviors are strongly oriented and shaped by cultural factors. All this shows, beyond any doubt, that THD is a serious regulating agent of human behaviors.

This type of analysis of the impact the THD on human behaviors is the common approach adopted by modern social sciences. It may be called *a cultural behaviorist approach*. The latter looks at the THD as external stimuli out there in the social milieu with little interest paid, if any, to the internal side of those stimuli. Behavioral psychologists are well known for their disdain for studying *the unobservable factors* which could affect human behavior. Their uneasiness with the disciplines of cognitive psychology (the study of the internal state of the human mind) and psychoanalysis (the study of the impact of unconsciousness on human behavior) appears to be associated with the study of the potential *hidden dimensions* of the THD like the transcendental features referred to earlier. For example, a review of the countless introductory books of sociology in the USA confirms the absence of reference to the transcendental dimensions of the THD. Most of these introductory textbooks have a chapter about culture where definitions of cultural concepts are given, explained, discussed, and sometimes applied. But despite of this, we don't recall yet having seen any of those many Introductory textbooks that have made reference to the transcendental dimensions of the THD (16).

This state of affairs could be accounted for by the general spirit of Western modern science. On the one hand, this science is more inclined to study the observable, the measurable, and the quantifiable phenomena. As such, it has a sort of *hostile attitude* toward those phenomena that don't qualify to be studied by the rather positivist approach. On the other hand, devising an appropriate new methodology becomes a big obstacle for those few *non-traditional* modern social scientists who recognize the legitimacy of those commonly non-observable, non-measurable, and non-quantifiable phenomena. In contrast to this, our interdisciplinary THD concept is potentially qualified to give importance to both objective and subjective dimensions of human parameters/determinants.

Social Sciences Unfit for the THD Study

The total failure of bio-genetical sciences to deal with the THD as such and the partial failure of modern social sciences to address the internal dimensions of the THD make both of them *unfit* to come to our help for comprehending *the THD from within.*

From a methodological viewpoint, there is a pressing need for the discovery of this 'hidden dimension' of the THD. We have established in the preceding pages that there is a strong correlation between THD and the human longer lifespan. In modern social sciences, correlation relationships between phenomena are usually interpreted in two ways: (1) Direct cause-effect relationship. This means one phenomenon is the direct cause of the other phenomenon. (2) Non-direct cause-effect relationship. This implies that the phenomenon in question is not caused by the other phenomenon in correlation, but rather by the so-called *intervening variable.* The latter is a factor/cause different from the phenomenon in correlation.

It could be said that both modern bio-genetical sciences and social sciences have, in general, remained *silent* on the direct or non-direct cause (s) which make (s) the growth and the full maturation of THD take much longer time in terms of the number of years than the growth and the full maturation of the organs of the human body. Social scientists are certainly aware of this factor. But one hardly can find in the vast social science literature the cause-effect or the intervening variable explanation(s) of this time difference in growth and maturation between the two realms of the human entity: the bio-physical human body and the THD. What one finds, instead, in this enormous social sciences literature is a 'descriptive approach' to statements and analysis. In other words, the THD is described as they could be observed and analyzed objectively and externally without making reference neither to why they grow slower or last longer (human ideas, thought) than the human bio-physical organs...nor do they consider the plausibility that the THD may have *'hidden dimension'* which is beyond the objective observable field of the Positivist science.

The Islamic Perspective as an Alternative

There is, therefore, a need for the adoption of an approach different from the prevailing conventional one in modern social sciences. It should be *a balanced approach. It studies the THD from within and from without.* It focuses equally on the external (the observable, the objective…) as well as the internal (subjective, transcendental…) dimensions of the THD. This approach belongs to what we called earlier *Inclusive Sociology.* In short, we need a perspective that could help us answer some of the questions about the THD that modern social sciences either have not raised or have not been interested in answering them. We have chosen the Islamic perspective for this task. There are three reasons for that. First, our interdisciplinary THD concept includes religious elements in its perspective. Second, we have been working on the THD for the last thirty years. The Islamic perspective is quite present in this work (17). Third, the Quran, Islam's Holy Book, is full of verses that speak of *dualism* as a common feature of all the universe's phenomena. From this point of view, the nature of the THD could not only be of a one-sided nature: external, objective, and observable. This view misses the inside hidden (subjective, the transcendental…) dimension of the nature of the THD. According to the Quran, the internal nature of the THD is heavily invested with the divine spark. Thus, modern social sciences' focus on the study of the THD from the outside is hardly objective scientifically. The credibility of the entire corpus of modern social sciences' concepts, theories, paradigms, etc. The THD will, therefore, be very much lacking. The inclusion of Islamic insights in the elaboration of our THD concept is part of making it interdisciplinary.

In using the Islamic perspective in the analysis of the THD, we have *two goals* in mind which are fully compatible with the thesis of this chapter: (1) The acquisition of more knowledge about *the internal nature of the THD.* As seen, they develop and mature much slower than the bio-physical human organs. Then, the legitimate question that should be raised is: What is in the THD that makes them slower in their development and maturation? (2) Could the findings from question (1) explain or make sense (Verstehen) of the strong correlation between the THD on the one hand, and the longer lifespan enjoyed by the members of the human species, on the other? The performance of the Islamic perspective in the exploration of the THD in the following pages is to be measured and tested by the kind of answers it will offer to these two major questions.

In Search for the Nature of the THD

The above brief description and analysis of the crucial role the THD may play in making of the human lifespan longer than those of the other species can be considered as a sort of positivist scientific description. That is, it confines itself to the description of tangible observations about THD and their potential impact on the longer human lifespan. This approach could hardly be sufficient to satisfy adequately the human curiosity and to articulate a solid understanding and explanation as to *why the THD is decisive in the promotion of a longer lifespan to the human species*. We need, therefore, to go beyond the mere descriptive approach of the THD and *raise substantial questions* about their very nature: What is the nature of the THD itself that enables it to act as a prolonger of the human lifespan? In other words, what is in them that delays, by many years, in comparison with other species, the full development and maturation of the organs of the human body? And what is in them as well that makes their own full-blown growth and maturation come at a later time of the humans' longer lifespan? These are not metaphysical philosophical questions (though our interdisciplinary THD concept allows well for philosophical inquiry). They are rather very realistic and down-to-earth questions which they have to be asked and attempts must be made in search of answering them. Because without doing so we hardly can hope to establish a solid and trustworthy knowledge of what makes us distinctly human (18).

What is quite clear here is that neither biology nor genetics could be of any great help to us as far as the understanding of the nature of the THD. The latter appears to constitute a world quite apart from the bio-physio-genetical world of the organs of the human body. The THD is not made up of bio-genetico-neuro-physiological elements like the human body. *The THD is super-organic* in Spencer's terminology. This may be one good plausible reason why they don't follow the same pace of development and maturation of the organs of the human body. In other words, the human entity is made up of *two realms* of different nature. Thus, what is needed, is the adoption of an approach suitable for the understanding of the nature of the THD.

This may require the modification or even the abandonment of the ethics and the main principles of the positivist approach adopted by modern Western science. What is most important in achieving credible science and knowledge is not the given adopted approach per se but rather the establishment of well-grounded understanding and explanation of the phenomena in question. We have chosen to use *the Islamic perspective* in our exploration of this apparent 'hidden' nature of the universe of the THD.

Human Nature in The Quran

In order to identify the nature of the THD from an Islamic perspective, we found no better reference than the Quran itself which is Islam's first authoritative reference text. There are many verses in the Muslim Holy Book that speak with clarity of human nature. We have chosen only *two verses* that describe in full the basic components of human nature. The two verses in question are: behold! thy Lord said to the angels: I am about to create man, from sounding clay from mud molded into shape. When 1 have fashioned him (in due proportion) and breathed into him of My spirit, fall ye down in obeisance unto him (19). Human nature, according to these two verses, is *dualistic* in nature. It is made up of clay and the divine-breathed spirit.

As to which one of these two components is more important in the making of human nature, one interpretation of these two verses may allow one to assert *that the Quran gives more importance to the side of the divine-breathed spirit into the human entity.* Since the angels were ordered by God to prostrate to Adam immediately *after*, and *not before*, the divine spirit was breathed into him. The angels' prostrating act before Adam is seen as a symbolic sign of respect to this godly new privileged creature who has been the only creature to receive *a special divine-breathed spirit*. This Quranic position in favor of the spiritual dimension of human nature is a fundamental permanent principle that runs throughout the entire text of the Quran. We are told again and again in the verses of the 114 Surahs of the Quran, that human individuals, groups, collectivities, societies, and civilizations can achieve excellence only when their divine breathed spirit *over dominates* the materialistic (clay) side of their human nature.

The Meaning of the Divine Spirit Among the Quran's Interpreters

The interpretation of the meaning of the verses of the Quran has been a major concern for Muslims in the past and in the present. We have chosen a very limited sample of the interpreters (al-Mufassirun) of the Quran who have done their work either in Arabic or in English. Fakrudine al-Razi who died in 1210 and Ahmad al-Ansari al-Qurtubi who died around 1293 are two well-known interpreters of the Quran of past Muslim civilization. There are also two widely used interpretations of the Quran which were written in Arabic in the last century by Said Qutb (an Egyptian) and Muhammad Tahar Ben Achour (a Tunisian). In English, there are today two famous interpretations of the Quran. Each one of them is considered a highly credible reference by English-speaking Muslims. The Indian Yusuf Ali and the Austrian Muhammad Assad are the authors of the two Quranic interpretations. Al-Razi (20) interpreted the word spirit (ruh) as wind which can be breathed in. Then, he admits that real knowledge of the divine spirit is not accessible to humans. As to al-Qurtubi's (21) interpretation of the word spirit, it is not very different from al-Razi's. For him, the spirit is like a wind and it has a gentile entity. As to the two contemporary Arab interpreters of the Quran, Said Qutb (22) speaks of the divine spirit as that breath that has enabled the human species to transcend its material (clay) make-up and reach out for the spiritual horizon where hearts and minds are in action. On his part, the Tunisian interpreter of the Quran Muhammad Tahar Ben Achour (23), sees the divine breath into Adam as a symbol of man's greatness in the eyes of God.

Yusuf Ali gives the following meaning to God's breath of spirit into man: the breathing of Allah's spirit into man, i.e., the faculty of *God-like knowledge and will* which, if rightly used, would give man superiority over other creatures (24). As to Muhammad Assad, he interprets the divine spirit this way: "God's 'breathing of His spirit' into man is obviously a metaphor for His endowing him with life and consciousness: that is, with a soul" (25).

These six interpretations of the word 'spirit' are generally *vague* as to the specific nature of the breathed divine spirit into man. Yusuf Ali's interpretation of the word spirit is perhaps the most tangible of all interpretations referred to here. As mentioned before, the word spirit meant for him God-like knowledge and will which were given only to man. It is an interpretation that attempts to avoid being entangled in the vagueness and generality reflected in the other interpretations. In other words, his interpretation of the breathed divine spirit as 'God-like, knowledge and will' invested in man could constitute one step toward helping identify more concretely the specific identity of the very nature of the breathed divine spirit into man.

The Operational Process of the Transcendental Spirit

The term 'the operational process' is used in modern social sciences to mean that social scientists should attempt to make vague phenomena and ideas more tangible. That is, quantifiable and measurable if possible. So the vague phenomena and ideas in question become operational and *empirically manageable*.

The operational process is certainly strongly inspired by the epistemology of Western modern science and knowledge. This epistemology relies heavily on its understanding and explanation of phenomena on identifiable, quantitative, and measurable variables and causes. The degree of success in the operational process varies from one category of phenomena to the other. For instance, the so-called subjective phenomena (personal feelings, opinions, etc.) are less easy to operationalize than the objective phenomena out there in the external world. Nonetheless, efforts must be made to identify as concretely as possible the hidden dimensions of vague phenomena.

As pointed out, the meaning of the divine spirit as conveyed by the six interpreters of the two Quranic verses remains rather vague. We need, therefore, to develop some sort of methodology that *could liberate us* from the use of vague and general labels which are of no help for a closer and more tangible understanding of the nature of the breathed divine spirit. In order to dissipate the obscurity surrounding the nature of the breathed divine spirit, we need to adopt *the following methodology*. First, we should identify objectively and in tangible terms those elements that really distinguish humans from the rest of the other species and make them superior to all of them. As mentioned earlier, the THD (language, thought, beliefs, science/knowledge, cultural norms, values, laws, etc.) is what distinguishes the human species most from other species. Second, the two Quranic verses referred to here speak also explicitly of man's distinct and prestigious status among all other creatures including the angels themselves who were asked by God to prostrate to Adam. The breathed-divine spirit appears to be behind the special place that was accorded to the human species on this planet/ and beyond. As indicated before, the angels' prostration of Adam came immediately after and not before the event of the divine breath took place in Adam.

Thus, the human objective analysis and the Quranic revealed text *concur* on human superiority over the other species. While the former relates it to the human species unique THD, the latter explains the human's distinct status by the breathed divine spirit into them. But there is hardly any contradiction between the two perspectives. The Quran consistently attributes humankind's distinct superiority over the other living species to its privileged THD as manifested in language use, science, thinking, learning, religion, laws, norms, moral ethics, etc.…In other words, both approaches point to *the crucial role of the THD in the making of human superiority/distinctiveness*. However, in the Quranic perspective, the divine-breathed spirit as a source of man's superiority/distinctiveness may have a broader meaning than the THD per se. That is, the broader meaning would cover everything that distinguishes humans from non-humans. The drawing below shows the kind of overlapping that exists between the THD and the divine-breathed spirit as the two determining factors of the superiority/distinctiveness of the human species. It remains, however, to be emphasized here the THD is the key factor in the divine breathed spirit for the human species overwhelming domination over the rest of the species.

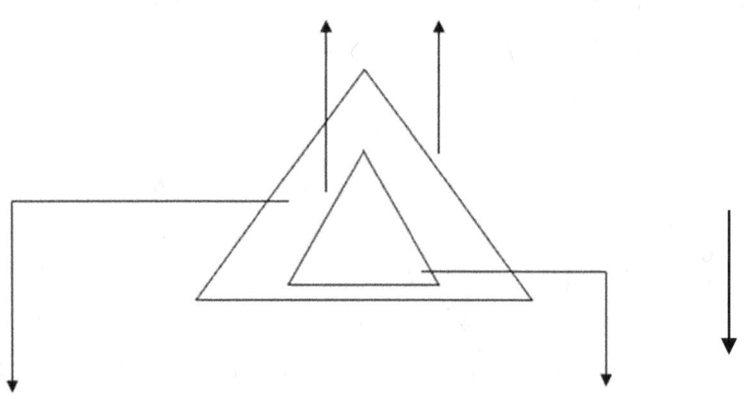

Our interdisciplinary operational analysis of the THD has so far clarified the broader nature of the divine-breathed spirit. The latter must, at least, include the THD. In other words, the divine-breathed spirit must be the THD or more than that. With this, the identity of the divine-breathed spirit is no longer as obscure as it was in the interpretations of the Quran's interpreters outlined earlier. So, in these Quranic verses, the word 'ruh' must first mean the THD. We see eye to eye with Dr Zaglul Annajar that Quran interpreters need credible scientific knowledge to convey the right meanings of the Quranic verses from both natural and social sciences(27).

The Nature of Divine Spirit

Having established that the THD, the larger part of the divine breathed spirit, does not stop our human curiosity from asking: What is exactly the divine spirit that the Quranic verses speak about as being breathed into man (Adam)? Of course, our interdisciplinary THD concept encourages us to raise substantive philosophical questions. We humans can hardly claim that we possess a precise answer to that very important question. As a first step toward getting closer to the answer, we need full knowledge of God's spirit. This appears to be beyond human reach. Many of the Quran's verses speak of our human knowledge limitations. « They ask thee concerning the spirit (of the inspiration), say: The spirit (cometh) by command of my Lord: Of knowledge, it is only a little that is communicated to you (28). »

On another level, the Quran states: « God is unique and, there is nothing whatever like unto Him (29). » So, neither can we compare His entity to what we know by our senses nor can we claim that we have a concrete idea about the nature of His spirit. Allah in the Ouran is the Absolute Transcendental. He is beyond any tangible human recognition and perception. "No vision can perceive Him. But His vision perceives everything: He is above all comprehension, yet is acquainted with all things" (30). He is often perceived by humans as a transcendental spirit and power that can only be vaguely imagined by humans. Modern science and past and contemporary philosophies are not of great help to us for an adequate knowledge of the divine entity and its spirit. On the one hand, modern science has almost completely avoided the issue of the divine presence on ideological as well as epistemological, and methodological bases. On the other hand, ancient philosophy remained generally metaphysical or mystical in its approach to the study of the divine, and some contemporary philosophers have gone as far as announcing God's death (31).

Thus, both revealed and human knowledge don't enable us to have tangible and precise ideas about the nature of God and His spirit.

The Manifestations of the Transcendental in the THD

Accepting that THD is the greater part of the breathed divine spirit as outlined in the Qur'anic text could hardly be an end in itself. We need to show how the transcendental breath is manifested in some of the THD. We present here *three manifestations* where the THD is found to reflect certain transcendental aspects of the dimensions of the divine breath.

The Long/Eternal Lifespan of the THD

In Islam, Allah is eternal. The Quranic verses express Allah's absolute eternity in this way: "He is the First and the Last" (32) or "All that is on earth will perish: But will abide (forever) the Face of thy Lord, full of Majesty, Bounty and Honor" (33). Thus, the long or eternal lifespan of the THD reflects some similarity with the divine trait of eternity. Let's take a brief look at how language, the mother of THD extends culturo-symbolically the lifespan of human collectivities and individuals.

As far as the language's capacity to perpetuate the cultural-symbolic heritage of human individuals, groups, and societies, there is plenty of evidence that attests to that. On the collective level, the written language enables human groups to record their collective memory and to preserve it and eternalize it inspite of their disappearance as bio-organic entities. The Arabic language's full maintenance of the Quranic text of the seventh century is a classical example of language's capacity to preserve for so long or forever the collective heritage and memory from the plausibility of destruction and annihilation that inevitably strikes the organic-physical-materialistic existence of those human collectivities.

Likewise, language enables individuals to survive culturally-symbolically their relatively short bio-organic existence. Well-known thinkers and writers of all human civilizations and of all ages could not have diffused and propagated in full their ideas, their theories, their paradigms, etc....had they not at their disposal a well-established language in their own culture. The ideas, theories, and laws of Plato, Aristotle, Ibn Khaldun, Ibn Rushd (Averoes), Rosseau, Marx, etc....could not have resisted the odds of time and space and lived for centuries or potentially forever without the help of the written languages. In short, linguistic systems permit the cultural heritage of people's memories as well as distinct thinkers' ideas to enjoy a great deal of long longevity or even eternity.

The new breakthroughs in the area of modern electronic techniques have particularly greatly improved quantitatively and qualitatively the humans' chance to perpetuate themselves in a kind of *metaphysical sense*. The codification process is a vivid example of THD's ability to eternalize the word, the voice, and the natural living image of living creatures as well as inanimate phenomena. The invention of the video is by far the perfect invention that fully enables humans to eternalize themselves culturally-symbolically. With it, it has become possible today to record in perfect and spontaneous manner the word, the voice's tonalities, and the movement of the individual's body. The late famous Egyptian singer, Oum Kalthoum, is no longer with us today. But she is still with us with the multiple and various poems she sang with her melodious voice and with her well-known Ahat (sad meditative loud voice). She is still, as she really was, with us with her white handkerchief standing before her crowded audience each first Thursday of the month of her singing season.

Freedom, Justice, and Equality's Transcendental Dimensions

The cultural values of freedom, justice, and equality constitute a second example illustrative of yet another type of THD transcendence. What we are precisely interested in here is to show how the impact of these cultural values on human behavior could galvanize it and transform it into a supernatural-like action.

Field observations of both the human species and the rest of the other living beings show, on the one hand, that the behavior of the latter is profoundly influenced by genetic and instinctive forces. And, on the other hand, human behavior is largely determined by the impact of THD. The power of the influence of genes and instincts on the behaviors of animals, birds, insects, etc....explains well *the persistent uniformity of their behaviors* that continues to prevail among successive generations throughout time and space. As far as the human species is concerned, there is a great variety in the patterns of major or minor behaviors that differentiate one civilization from another, one society from another, and one generation from another. There is a strong consensus among modern sociologists and anthropologists that those differences in the patterns of behaviors are basically due to the impact of the THD like religions, traditions, cultural values and norms, systems of knowledge, myths, etc....that exist in those human social gathering (34). In other words, the THD allows humans to have access to freedom of action, choice, and difference from the other(s).

On this basis, human behavior enjoys a great deal of flexibility. That is, it is governed by *a docile determinism* and not by a rigid determinism like the case with the behavior of the rest of the living species. It is no surprise, from this point of view to see the predictions of human behaviors by specialists fail in many cases. Modern psychologists and sociologists often tend to ground their expected predictions of human behaviors on *a rigid deterministic basis* whose laws hardly recognize the principles of human freedom, will, and choice...in the equation of potential influences on human behaviors (35). It is of great importance here to draw attention to the fact that the cultural values of freedom, justice and other human universal values that humans have sought throughout their very long scientific interest history *have hardly been examined with any serious effort on the part of positivist social scientists*. The latter appear to have considered such cultural values as philosophical in nature. Thus, they ought to be rejected outright. Accordingly, they don't deserve a profound exploration as to their impact on the shaping of human behaviors. They are seen as metaphysical notions that interest philosophers and not Positivist social scientists. *The shortcomings of their approach* will persist as long as they deal with human behaviors as completely free from the effect of subjective, transcendental, and cultural symbolic factors (36).

The humans' remarkable distinctness with the traits of freedom, the sense of justice, the ability to choose…*brings them closer to the metaphysical world*. In most religions and faiths, gods are seen to be privileged with those characteristics. As such, it is only the human being who relatively shares those qualities with gods. As explained before, the Quranic text makes a direct allusion to that human transcendental link which is the basis, according to the Quran, of freedom, will, and the ability to choose…on the part of humans. The origin of all that comes from the divine breath into human nature…« So, when I have made him and breathed into him of *My spirit*, do ye (angels) fall down, prostrating ourselves unto him (37). With that generous divine gift, the human being becomes the most qualified being on earth to take up the full responsibility of its management. » "We offered our trust to the heavens, to the earth, and to the mountains, but they refused the burden and were afraid to receive it. man undertook to bear it, but he has proved a sinner and a fool" (38).

Neither the world of the other living species nor that of artificial intelligence machines have the quantity and the quality of the THD. It is an utter non-realism to speak of the meanings of freedom, equality, and justice…among other living species as they have been debated by the human species throughout the centuries. The decisive and crucial factor that radically separates humans from both the world of AI machines and non-human living creatures is the set of THD. It is on the basis of the latter that derives the legitimacy of conceiving the transcendence of the human identity. Without taking into account the impact of the world of the THD on human behavior, we hardly can expect to formulate an articulate understanding of the nature of humans and their relationships with what surrounds them here on earth or what stimulates their imagination over there in the sky.

What has taken place on the political and social fronts late last century in Eastern Europe and the former Soviet Union constitutes a genuine illustration of the transcendental nature of human cultural values as the THD. The changes in the political systems in the second half of the year 1989 and in the Summer of 1990 in both the Socialist Eastern European societies and the former Soviet Union could not be easily understood without reference to the mobilizing effect of the THD on the behaviors of social actors. The call by various groups for the democratization of those totalitarian political regimes was meant to signal the desire for ending the state of siege surrounding the exercise of freedom as a cultural symbolic value. It could be said that the politico-social practices of those dictatorial regimes go against the principle that stipulates *that humans are by nature cultural symbolic beings*. That is, they hardly could accept in the long run the death of their cultural symbolic instinct.

As argued before, the THD is the main source that generates diversity and differences among human individuals and groups. By its nature, it is hostile to any repressive homogenization which attempts to make individuals and societies identical to each other. Modern socialist and communist countries' policies are at odds with this. The prohibition of striking in the factory, traveling outside the national frontiers, establishing political parties, speaking freely, criticizing, expressing opposite views, protesting, etc….are practices that are in conflict with what the THD are intrinsically predisposed to promote. The exclusion of humans from practicing their freedom in the largest sense of the term will ultimately lead to being very similar to both the world of non-human living creatures and that of AI machines.

Our concept of social actors as cultural symbolic beings *first* is in clear contradiction with the assumptions of historical materialism (39). The ideology of the political regimes of the socialist and communist societies advocates that humans are first of all materialistic/economically oriented in nature. Everything else in human nature is either secondary in importance or of false basis. This materialistic perception of humans has led to the marginalization or worse to the annihilation of the role of the THD in the shaping of human behavior. This is true, especially among extreme and rigid materialist Marxist thinkers.

The THD's Weightless and Shapeless Nature

As already stressed, the considerable easiness by which the THD can be brought and diffused through space is to be essentially attributed to the substantial non-presence of certain tangible parameters that the non-THD often have. Weight, physical and material shape constitute the basic tangible parameters of solid and material things and they make up the major obstacles for carrying and diffusing them easily from one place to another. As for the THD, it is intrinsically *weightless* and *shapeless*. Their speedy mobility, instant movement, carrying, and diffusion from one place to another are to be explained by their fundamental weightless and shapeless nature. As such, as long as the THD is kept weightless and shapeless, its transportation and diffusion will be much easier and much faster. For instance, the THD has weight and shape when it is written in print which has physical material weight and shape. To carry heavy encyclopedias, books, documents, newspapers, magazines, journals, and so on through space will take a long time and a great effort if the distance is e far away and the means of transportation are primitive. Modern means of transportation have certainly improved the speed and reduced the amount of hardship in carrying and transporting even the heaviest physical material things from one place to another. But the *weight-shape factor* of things remains, nonetheless, a crucial factor as far as the fast mobility of things and the physical work put into their moving. This point becomes clear when shape and weight variables are dropped altogether from the scene of the transmission of the THD. That is, when the THD regains its shapeless and weightless initial intrinsic state. The invention of fax and other electronic means has done just that. Small and large written documents can be sent today and with very little effort to reach instantly the farthest points on the globe Obviously, this is made possible by the elimination of the weight and shape *variables* of the written print material in which the THD used to be sent to a given destination.

The shapeless and weightless characteristics of the nature of the THD appear to move them far away from the logic and the rules that govern the universe of the physical material things that have weight and shape and put them, instead, *in the orbit of spiritual and transcendental beings which are assumed to be shapeless and weightless.* This state of being without weight and shape appears to leave no room for any constraint that could block the free and instant movement of the THD. The silent communication through telepathy, oral communication by telephone, the written communication by fax and the Internet are all instant communications between the parties involved. This occurs despite the enormous physical material obstacles like deserts, mountains, seas, and oceans which may separate the communicating parties. These several types of communication from a distance have one thing in common: They are *absolutely free* from the constraints of weight and volume.

Our examination of these three different manifestations shows that the THD has features that make them resemble significantly spirits and supernatural beings. This is strongly compatible with the Quranic view on the origin of the THD. In a nutshell, they are part of the special divine breath which Adam had received. The mixing of the divine breath with the clay in Adam's creation *had established for ever human duality: matter and spirit.* The above discussion of the three manifestations underlines that the THD is heavily impregnated with the divine/the transcendent side of human duality.

The discussion just elaborated on the transcendental manifestations of THD shows well that our THD concept is strongly interdisciplinary. We have used both social and human sciences (anthropology, sociology, political science, religion, philosophy) to deal with the issues at hand.

The Image of Man in the Quran

So far, we have established two major observations:

1. There is a strong correlation between the THD and the longer human lifespan.
2. From the Quranic viewpoint, the THD is of divine origin. Consequently, it shows transcendental manifestations in human action.

The question now is this: is it possible to rely on these two observations in order to account for the longer human lifespan? The Islamic perspective has its own view of the creation of man as well as his image in the world of countless living species. First, the Quran offers its version of Adam's creation. This is spelled out in full in many verses of the Quran. The event of the human creation was the outcome of the interaction between the physical (the clay) and the metaphysical (the breathed-divine spirit). In other words, human creation was the result of a contact between matter and the divine spirit.

Second, the Quranic text addresses the consequences of the event of human creation. That is, what did happen when the fusion between matter and the divine spark took place? As an answer to such a question; the Quran speaks highly of the new creature *(Adam)*; because the matter (the clay) is no longer just a matter. It is now part of the divine spirit. In modern terms, the new creature is no longer a purely quantitative (matter/clay) being. With the breathed-divine spirit in him, he is now a *qualitative creature* as well.

Third, the Quranic text does not only point out explicitly to these two poles of the human entity but *it sides strongly*, at the same time, more *with man's qualitative dimension* whose origin is the divine spirit. As mentioned before, the divine order to the angels to prostrate to Adam came after, and no**t** before, the divine spirit was breathed into the new creature: "When I have fashioned him (in due proportion) and breathed into him of My spirit, fall ye down in obeisance unto him." In Quranic terms, the most important dimension of the dualistic human entity is that one which directly resulted from the breathed-divine spirit. This is in full logic with the Quranic epistemology. In the Quran, God is the ultimate of the ultimate in wisdom, knowledge, creation, action, mercy, and perfection. So, a little spark of His spirit breathed into Adam in clay shape is bound to radically transform the quality of that dead-shaped clay. This great transformation has not only made man the master over the rest of the other creatures but also God's representative (khalifa) on this planet. He is superior over other species not because of his quantitative dimension (physical size, height, etc....) but basically because of his qualitative dimension: the special set of the THD. This is the overwhelming position of today's social and human sciences. (40)

Dualistic Human Entity and Longer Lifespan

How does this Quranic dualistic image of man help explain the longer human lifespan? It has been emphasized throughout this chapter that humans live longer because their THD develops and matures slower than the bio-physical organs of the human body. As such, humans need to live longer in order for their THD could achieve their full development and maturity. How can we use the Quranic dualistic view of man to account for the human longer lifespan?

In order to answer this fundamental question, we confine ourselves to the use of our concept of the THD as elaborated in this chapter and this book. On the other hand, we use a Quranico-metaphysical-philosophical vision to help understand and explain how the THD could play a decisive role in the making of a longer human lifespan. This approach is anti-positivist in nature. There should be no surprise in the adoption of such a vision. It is argued throughout this chapter that the THD is heavily impregnated with transcendence. The latter can hardly be accepted let alone be studied, by empirical positivist science. We would like to discuss the relationship between THD and the human's longer lifespan away from the narrow logic of strict empiricism and positivism, but within our adopted interdisciplinary perspective. The THD has transcendental features. The transcendental universe is different from the five senses human experience world. *The transcendental universe has its own logic, rules, and dynamics.* Our Quranico-metaphysical-philosophical approach is greatly free from the constraints of empiricism and positivism. The latter are ill-equipped for the study of the transcendence of the THD. The discussion of the THD here is beyond the reach of positivist science.

Using our interdisciplinary approach, we confine ourselves here to the discussion of *four ideas/hypotheses* about the links between THD and the longer human lifespan.

1. It could be argued that THD grows and matures slower because its nature *is more* complex than the nature of the bio-physical organs of the human body. In the words of Cassirer, "man is compensated by another gift which he alone develops and which bears no analogy to anything in organic nature. Not immediately but by a very complex and difficult process of thought, he arrives at the idea of abstract space" (41). So, humans need to live longer because the complexity of their THD requires more time for the realization of full development and maturity of the complex of the THD. While the complexity assumption is acceptable as a tangible and objective tool for analysis of the correlation between THD and the longer human lifespan, it does not, however, put an end to many of the questions that could be raised in this regard. For instance, what do we mean by the complexity of the THD? What makes them more complex than the bio-

physical organs of the human body? Are they more complex because of their metaphysical/divine origin? The answers to these questions are hard to be sought within the framework of empirical-positivist science. What is needed here is a perspective that sheds light and improves our understanding of phenomena in which empiricism and positivism can practically offer no help. Interdisciplinary insights from religion, philosophy, and metaphysics should be, therefore, welcomed as long as they bring us closer to the understanding of the nature of the THD and its special impact on the behavior and destiny of the human species.

2. The correlation between THD and the longer human lifespan could be examined within **a** parapsychological framework. That is, how spirit affects matter. The Quranic version of Adam's creation is a classical example of the interaction between matter and spirit. Adam is the outcome of the combination of the clay and the divine spirit. As pointed out, the breathed-divine spirit had transformed the quality of the new human being. The divine spark had endowed him with transcendental characteristics. We have shown how the THD is heavily impregnated with transcendentality. It could also be argued here that the THD does not have only longer/eternal lifespan in itself, but it also *transfers* this quality to matter. That is, the human body's lifespan is extended. There appears to be an unavoidable mutual influence between spirit and matter once they are fused together in one entity like Adam's. So, the side effect of the THD longer/eternal lifespan is carried *in a limited manner*, so to speak, to the bio-physical side (clay, matter) of the human entity. The parapsychological view of the longer human lifespan could hardly be in disagreement with the religio-philosophical-metaphysical insights about the role of the THD on human destiny (42).

3. As seen before, the THD is the greater important part of the breathed divine spirit into man. It is part of what we have called the qualitative dimension of the dualistic humane entity. From a Quranic point of view, the divine spirit, including especially the THD is the best side of man's duality. Without the divine spirit, man could not have been God's only representative on earth. But this has its own consequences. As it has been emphasized, the full development and maturation require a longer time. In other words, humans have to pay a price for the gift of the enormous use of THD.

   The price here is time in years and decades which the full development of both their human body and their THD would necessarily need. But this price has its positive aspects. It has allowed humans to have a longer lifespan. There is no doubt that the THD is at the core of man's qualitative dimension. There is, therefore, a strong need for more time in years and decades to pay for that qualitative side. So, the full development and maturation of the entire human entity would be materialized. As such, the longer human lifespan *ought not* be only examined through bio-genetic determinism but it deserves to be analyzed as well by the culturo-religio-philosophico-metaphysical insights.

4. From a Quranic point of view, the origin of the longer human life is the breathed-divine spirit in humans. There are two manifestations of this. On the one hand, as shown in the preceding pages, there is a strong correlation between longer human lifespan and the presence of THD among the members of the human species. The THD takes a much longer time (in years and decades) to see itself reach its peak in growth, development, and maturation. This has made humans enjoy longer lifespans as compared with the shorter lifespans of the members of the other living species. That is, the impact here of THD on the lengthening of the human lifespan is a limited one.

On the other hand, the Quranic text is quite explicit that the breathed-divine spirit had endowed man to become ultimately *an eternal being*. Of course, he is not bio-physically eternal in this world. He just lives a longer life than the other species. But he is eternal after the resurrection. According to the Quran, he will live forever in paradise or hell. There is no mention in the Quranic text either of the resurrection of non-human species or their eternal life afterward. This difference between humans and non-humans in the length of lifespan in this world and in the eternal life after resurrection appears to be strongly related to the special divine spirit that only humans have received, according to the Quran. This divine spirit has made man both God's khalifa in this world and accountable for his actions in front of God who will examine the humans' accountability on the Day of Judgment after which humans will live forever in paradise or hell. As argued throughout this long chapter, the THD is an outstanding component of the breathed divine spirit. It is a decisive force for the longer lifespan of humans and because of them, humans are also held responsible for their actions in this life for which they receive either eternal life in paradise or hell. In other words, the THD can be seen first as the main force behind the relatively longer human lifespan and, second, as, the principal factors, from a Quranic viewpoint, that make humans legitimate for eternal life after the resurrection. Thus, the correlation between THD and the lifespan of human existence appears to be strong both in *the relative and the absolute sense* of the length of lifespan.

The late great Egyptian thinker Abdulwahhab Elmessiri wrote me a letter in 1998 where he made the following remarks on the link between the THD and the longer human lifespan: "your concept of the THD and the human longer lifespan is certainly a pioneering concept. Establishing a relation between the two is something that does not initially come to one's mind. As such, your concept constitutes a breakthrough in modern science"

References and Notes

1. Bly, B. M., and Rumechatt, D. (1999) (eds), *Cognitive Science*, San Diago, Academic Press,.

2. Bonnell, V., and Hunt, L. (1999) (eds), *Beyond the Cultural Turn*, Berkeley, University of California Press.

3. Baert, P. (1998) *Social Theory in The Twentieth Century*, New York, New York University Press, p.1.

4. *The World Almanac and Book of Facts* 1994, p.175.

5. Wilson, E. (1975) *Sociobiology:The New Synthesis*, Cambridge, Mass, Harvard University Press.

6. *Time Magazine*, March 6, 1995, p.45, and *Al Wassat Magazine* (in Arabic) March 6, 1995, p.68.

7. *Time Magazine*, op.

8. Ibid.

9. Morin, E. (1990) *Introduction à la pensée complexe*, Paris, E. S. F.

10. Gardner, h. (1982) *Art, Mind and Brain: A Cognitive Approach to Creativity*, New York, Basic Books, Inc, p.357 and Hunt, M. (1982) *The Universe Within: A New Science Explores the Human Mind*, New York, Simons and Schuster, p.279.

11. *Encyclopedia of Psychology*, The Dushkin Publishing Group, Inc. Guilford, Conn. USA 1973, p.43.

12. Ibid.

13. This strong correlation between the THD and longer lifespan is found in the following study: Attendance at cultural events, reading books or periodicals, and making music or singing in a choir as determinants for survival: Swedish interview survey of living conditions, *British Medical, Journal*, vol.313, 21–28, December1996, pp.1577. Conclusion: attendance at cultural events may have a positive influence on survival and mortality.

14. Morin, E., op.

15. Rischer, C. E., and Easton, Th. A. (1992) *Focus on Human Biology*, New York, Harper Collins Publishers Inc., p.603.

16. White, L. (1973) *The Concept of Culture*, Edina, Alpha Edition.

17. Dhaouadi, M. (1996) *Toward Islamic Sociology of Cultural Symbols*, Kuala Lumpur, A. S. Noordeen.

18. Contemporary anthropology and sociology are the two disciplines that have studied culture more than any other discipline in the social and human sciences. But both have failed to ask and especially to answer those kinds of questions about the very deep internal nature of culture. Some of the few anthropologists and sociologists who came a little close to those questions and answers ended up using vague and confusing terms that have kept anthropology and sociology at a distance from dealing with the substantive and profound nature of culture. For those few, culture is seen as super-organic, supra-biological, an abstraction, as having no ontological reality or belonging to an extrasomatic context (see *The Concept of Culture*, op. pp.47,10,24,29).

19. *The Quran*: 15: 28–29.

20. Al-Razi, F. (1981) '*Tafsir Al Qur'an*' (in Arabic), Beirut, Dar Al Fikr, X, 185–186.

21. Al-Qurtubi, Abou Abdullah, *Al Jamia Li-Ahkam al Qur'an* (in Arabic), Cairo, Dar al Kitab al Arabi li Ahiba'awa al Nnashri, 1967, X,24–25.

22. Qutub, S. (1985) *Zilal al Qur'an* (in Arabic) Beirut, Dar al Shark, Vol. XII, X, IIVB, pp.21,35,39.

23. Ben Achour, M. T., *Tafsir Al Tahrir wa al Tanwir* (in Arabic), Tunis, Dar al Tunisiyah li-Annashr, vol.XIII (no date), pp.43–47.

24. Ali, A. Y. (1989) *The Meaning of The Holy Qur'an*, Brentwood, Maryland, (USA), Amana Corporation, 1989, Surah XV, 28–29, p.625.

25. Assad, M., *The Message of the Qur'an*, Gibraltar, Dar Al-Andalus, p.386.

26. The French monthly magazine *"Sciences Humaines"* has made a recent brief review (No.139, June 2003, pp.16–24) of research on human nature from the point of view of Evolutionary Psychology (EP). It is shown that EP has two versions of human nature:

   (a)   The hard version sees human instincts as programs of rigid and very specific univariable rigid behaviors (p.23).

   (b)   The soft or moderate version believes that human nature does exist, but it expresses itself in terms of propensities, potentialities, inclinations, and tendencies rather than in terms of rigid programs (p.23). Obviously, this version gives a large role to culture in the determination of human behaviors. As such, it does not come close to our concept of the centrality of the THD (culture) in the making of human nature itself. That special strong centrality of THD does not only greatly determine human behaviors but also the bio-physical destiny (longer lifespan) of humans as argued in this chapter.

27. Annajar, z. (2002) *The Quran's Scientific Inimitability* (in Arabic), Part I, Shorouk International Library, Cairo, Third Edition.

28. *The Quran 17:85.*

29. *The Quran: 42:11.*

30. *The Quran*: 6:106.

31. The German philosopher Nietsches (1844–1900) is a classical example.

32. *The Quran*: 57:3.

33. *The Quran*: 55:26–27.

34. Smelser, N., Smelser, W. (1967) *Personality and Social Systems*, New York, John Wiley and Sons, Inc., pp.80–87.

35. Philips, D. C. (1985) *Philosophy, Science and Social Inquiry*, New York, Pergamon Press.

36. The French Social determinist sociologist Emile Durkheim and the Behaviorist American psychologist BF Skinner are leading figures in modern behavioral social sciences in their opposition to non-objective factors as determinants of human behaviors.

37. *The Quran* 15:28–29.

38. *The Quran* 33:72.

39. Balibar, E. (1979) *Cinq Etudes du Matérialisme Historique*, Paris, Maspéro.

40. Dortier, J.-F. (2004) *L'homme cet étrange animal*, Auxerre Cedex, Sciences Humaines Editions, 398 pp.

41. Cassirer, E. (1970) *An Essay on Man*, New York, Bantam Books, p.48.

42. Pedler, K. (1981) *Mind Over Matter: A Scientific View of The Paranormal*, London, Thames Methuen.

Chapter V
'The Third Human Dimension' Paradigm: A New Intellectual Framework for the Promotion of Cultural Sociology

Introduction

This chapter strongly argues that humans are intrinsically *cultural beings*. This is the feature that distinguishes most of the human species from the rest of the species, as outlined in the preceding chapters. This unique human characteristic is manifested in the following cultural symbols/CS: knowledge, language, thought, religion, laws, myths, cultural values, and norms. In this chapter/ like in the others, the THD is equivalent to the term 'the Third Human Dimension'/ THD. As already mentioned, this stems from *our new conceptualization of the human identity*. We conceive the latter as made of body, soul, and the CS. So, CS is the THD of the human identity. This is different from the common view of the human identity as a dual identity made of (body and soul). As such, we consider the human identity as *a tri-dimensional identity*.

We adopt *a different methodology* in support of the thesis of this chapter which stipulates that humans are tri-dimensional creatures. This methodology uses both reason and Islamic religious insights to present its argument in favor of the THD as a special distinctive feature of the human species. In Arabic and Islamic intellectual culture, this methodology is called the *Aql/reason* and *Naql/religious* methodology.

That is, it combines both the use of the analysis of the mind/reason and the insights of the Islamic religious perspective on the issues and phenomena under consideration. Because the intense focus here is on the THD, we like to call the adopted view *a Third Human Dimension Paradigm*. Ibn Khaldun's social thought in his *Muqaddimah* strongly adopts the Aql-Naql perspective. One telling example is sufficient to make the point. He links the phenomenon of what he calls 'excessive sedentary culture and luxury' to the weakening, the disintegration, and the ultimate fall of society and civilization. This is clearly spelled out in section 18 of chapter 4 of the *Muqaddimah*. Ibn Khaldun supports his observations by citing the Quran. He writes: "If this situation spreads in a town or a nation, God permits to be ruined and destroyed. This is the meaning of the word of God: When we want to destroy a village, we order those of its inhabitants who live in luxury to act wickedly therein. Thus, the word becomes true for it, and we do destroy it" (Ibn Khaldun 1974:287).

Cultural Sociology

Three major recently published books focus on cultural sociology. They underline the emerging important role of culture in American sociological studies as Smith states, "Over the past ten to fifteen years 'culture' has developed to become one of the most popular and important areas within sociology in the United States" (Smith 1998:1). As to its definition, American cultural sociologists define this new sub-discipline as dealing with *meaning-making* which is implicitly assumed as the outcome of the cultural dimension of humans (Spillman 2007:1, Alexander 2012:22). This chapter attempts to deal with cultural sociology from a different and a new perspective (Dhaouadi 2013). Before doing this, let us have a summary review of the concept of culture in contemporary social sciences.

Models of Culture

An entire chapter titled (Models of Culture) has made a full review of the concept of culture in contemporary social sciences (Kincaid 2012:387–408). The author of this chapter (Risjord) has covered various aspects related to culture: the origins of the culture concept, culture and meaning, structure, agency, and emotion, the Neo-Bosnian Model, the Epidemiological Model, and the Practice Theory. Risjord's review emphasizes that *culture is an external feature of human societies*. That is, something that exists out there in societies having no innate prior present aptitudes in human nature. Tylor's classical definition of culture is a telling example: "Culture or civilization, taken in its wide ethnographic sense, is that complex whole which includes knowledge, belief, art, morals, law and any other capacities and habits acquired by man as a member of society" (Kincaid 2012:389). The conceptualization of culture as a societal feature allows Tylor and others like Kroeber and Sapir to explain differences between human groups. Tylor's scientific goal was to make sense of human diversity by which human communities were classified as lower or higher at the stages of the scheme of evolution (Kincaid 2012:389–390).

Culture as a Third Human Dimension

As shown in the proceeding chapters, our long research on the concept of culture has gone through many stages which ended by *giving culture a new name called the Third Human Dimension/ THD*. Epistemologically, the THD is conceptualized in our framework as an explicit manifestation of *prior innate* human aptitudes. The birth of the THD has a story that deserves to be told to see how concepts and theories could potentially be born on the agenda of doing *Basic Research* in social sciences. We believe it is worth reminding the reader by retelling him/her the story of my discovery of the concept/theory of the THD. This is highly relevant to the promotion of the skill of theorizing in social sciences as called for by the sociologist Richard Swedberg in his book (*The Art of Social Theory* 2014).

Following my return to Tunisia, my home country, after my studies and teaching in North America as well as other countries, I began my so-called serious course of thinking and research in attempting *to build a sort of paradigm* in order to understand human nature, behaviors and the dynamics of human societies within the perspectives of sociology and psychology. I adopted the next steps in order to attempt to get close to or fulfill that goal:

1. My intellectual curiosity has proposed and encouraged me to work out a coherent intellectual framework based on sociological and psychological insights that might help understand and explain people's behaviors and the dynamics of human societies and civilizations. I told myself with adequate trust and optimism that *the task* in question *was not an impossible one.*

2. I continued this self-dialogue with courage raising this methodological question: *Where* should I start to explore the puzzle of human nature, human behaviors, and the dynamics of human societies? The answer to this question has expressed itself this way: I must start *first of all* by identifying *the special traits* that distinguish the human species from the rest of the species. Because I believed that the discovery of these traits puts the course of my research on good grounds: at *square one.* I strongly thought that these traits were very suitable for a credible trustworthy understanding and explanation of people's behaviors and the dynamics of human groups and societies.

3. I have found fit to use in my research *the Third Human Dimension/ THD* (language, thought, knowledge, science, religion, laws, myths, cultural values, and norms) which distinguish the human species from the other species. The naming of this dimension as *the third one* of human nature is appropriate because the human entity—according to my new conceptualization—is made of *three features* (body, soul, and

THD). Thus, it has become clear to me that the profound study of THD is *the crux of the matter* for the understanding and explanation of human behaviors and societal phenomena.

4. Then, I asked: which element of the THD is the decisive and crucial one in the birth and making of the entire THD system among humans? *Language* in its spoken and written forms was my answer to this question. Thus, I describe *language* as *the Mother* of all human symbols making the THD. Because we hardly can imagine the existence of parts of the THD like religion, science, thought, etc....without the presence of language *first*.

This gives legitimacy to call human beings *linguistic-cultural beings* by nature. That is, the human being is not only a speaking being as described by ancient and modern philosophers and social thinkers but he/she is also at the same time a great user of the components of the THD. As such, one can imitate Descartes' Cogito and state: *I use language, therefore, I am human.* In other words, humans acquire the unique characteristics of being human with the full THD qualities by the use of the gift of language in its oral form, at least.

Basic Observations on Human Distinctiveness

Following the above four observations, I come now to the substance of certain ideas which enforce the thesis of the THD. These ideas have allowed me to make out of the concept of the THD *a theoretical perspective.* The latter is based on a set of potential innovative and unusual personal research observations on five features that distinguish the human species from the rest of the species on the planet.

The assumptions that 'humans are culturally symbolic/ THD beings by nature' are based on *a* set of five observations. To my knowledge, the centrality of THD in the human identity, as illustrated earlier and in the drawing below, may utterly be *new and innovative* in contemporary social sciences. Here is how I have been led to develop this fresh conceptualization of the centrality of the THD/culture in the human identity (Homo Culturus):

1. The process of the human body's growth and maturation is *slow* compared with those of other living beings. For instance, on average, human babies begin walking at the age of one year, while animal babies may walk right away or within a few hours or days after their birth.
2. In general, humans have *longer lifespans* than most animals.
3. The human race has an uncontested *dominant role* on earth and beyond.
4. Humans are privileged by *the THD.*
5. As stated before, the human identity is made up of *three parts*: the body, the soul, and the THD. Thus, it is fully a *tri-dimensional identity* while it is often referred to in religions and philosophy as a dual identity made of body and soul.

The THD Insightful Explanation

The slow human body growth and maturation could be explained by the fact that human entire growth and maturation involve *two fronts*: The body front and that of the THD. In short, the growth and maturation of non-human species are *uni-dimensional* (body) because of their lack of THD in the most complex human sense of the term. In contrast, the growth and maturation of humans are *bi-dimensional*. They involve two levels: the body level and the THD level. So, this two-level process is seen by this author's hypothesis to be behind the human slow body growth and maturation. That is, the process of the human body growth and maturation is slowed down, so to speak, among humans because humans are involved in *a second process* of growth and maturation represented by the THD. This interpretation might have *an insightful quality* and might have a lot of novel spirit. The following drawing describes *the central position* and role of the THD in the making of the human identity.

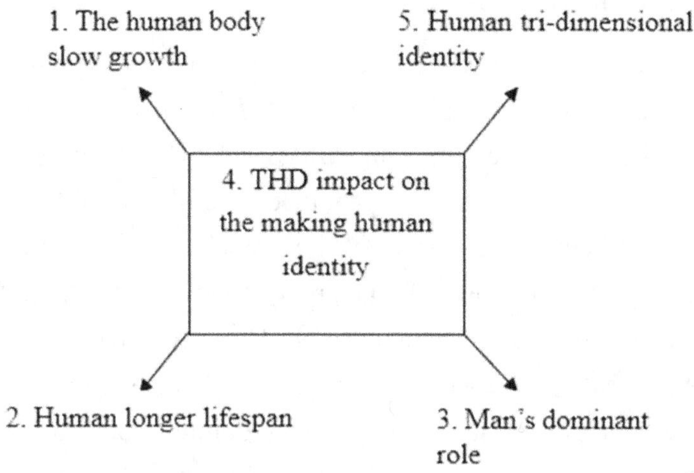

The THD is Not Central to Social Sciences

There is almost total silence on the centrality of the THD in the human identity in contemporary social sciences. Economists and those who have a materialist view have described man as Homo Oeconomicus. On their part, political scientists and those interested in political issues have labeled man as Homo Politicus. As to sociologists, they see the human being as a very social being or Homo Sociologus. Because of the present increasing use of numbers today, some have called man a Homo Numericus (Compiègne 2011:25). However, despite their great interest in the study of culture, contemporary anthropologists have hardly used terms related to culture to describe man as first of all *a HomoCulturus* (White 1973:29). So came the absence in Latin of the term 'Culturus'. This marginalization of the importance of culture/ THD and its central and decisive role in helping to understand and explain human phenomena is a marginalization that is likely *to damage* the credibility of these social sciences. Consequently, *present social sciences can hardly secure theoretically and empirically good understanding and explanation* of the human and social phenomena without giving a central role to the THD/culture in their making.

Man: The Non-Homo Culturus

The special issue of the French review Science & Avenir (Jan–Feb 2012:61) has asked 100 eminent scientists from natural as well as social sciences the following question: Qu'est-ce que l'Homme?: What is Man? None of the answers has provided a definition of man as first of all a cultural being. The answer of the French sociologist Edgar Morin is no exception. Because of his great interest in the complexity of phenomena, Morin labels man as *Homo Complexus* (p.62).

The general negligence of the major importance of culture is hardly new in contemporary social sciences as pointed out before. The pre-1960 theorists of culture like Weber, Durkheim, Marx, Parsons, Mills, Communists, Fascists, and others are known to have had a *'weak program'* for the importance of culture in their published works. In other words, they gave culture minor importance in their analysis (Semashko, Daloz, Erdemir 2006:831–838). Furthermore, the Birmingham School, Bourdieu, Foucault, and the theory of production and consumption of culture have not done better on their part: they have adopted a 'weak program' in the study of culture. The 'weak program' trend still dominates sociological studies of culture today even though the 'strong program' (giving culture a first importance) of cultural sociology is gaining more attention, especially among some American sociologists, as mentioned earlier in some other chapters, and since the birth of the so-called 'cultural turn' in the late 1990s(Wolff 1999:503).

The 'weak program' that sociologists have adopted for the study of culture may be explained, in part, by what Alain Touraine considers sociologists' negligence to focus on *social actors*. Touraine claims that sociologists tend to be interested in the study of systems like industrial and capitalist societies. He argues that contemporary thought has minimized *the subjective side* of social actors as Marx, Freud, and Nietzsche had done (Wieviorka 2007:25–27). Touraine stresses the importance for social sciences *to combine* the social system and the social actors in their analysis to understand and explain social action in society, "It is neither excessive nor paradoxical to say that the idea of society is a major obstacle which bothers the development of social sciences because they are based on the separation and even the opposition between the system and the social actors, while the idea of society implies their direct link" (Wieviorka 2007:28).

THD Link with the Word 'Read' in the Quran

It is well known and established that the Quran's revelation *started* by addressing the prophet Mohammad with the verb *'read'* in the Quran verse, "read in the name of your Lord" (96:1). One might raise here the question: Is there wisdom behind beginning the divine revelation by the verb 'read' in the imperative tense? Instead, the revelation could have also addressed the Prophet in this first encounter by other verbs like 'trade in the name of your Lord' or 'cultivate the land in the name of your Lord'. Was the start of the divine revelation with the verb 'read' a plain coincidence or was it founded on the divine full wisdom?

Social Psychology's Insights

Social psychology, in particular, could shed some insights on the profound meaning of the divine first address to the Prophet by the verb 'read'. Social psychologists give a lot of credit to the importance of the first impressions people have of each other in their first meetings. These impressions are expected *to stick better and last much longer in people's memories*. Based on this assumption, the first thing to be mentioned by the divine revelation to the prophet Mohammad in the first encounter with him in the cave/cavern of Heraa must be of *extreme importance* to the residents of Mecca and humanity at large. As such, the verb 'read' qualifies to be much more significant than the other verbs to the entire humankind. The verb 'read' is most important to the wide opening of the gates of knowledge and its horizons. That is, *the verb 'read' makes humans full cultural beings different* from the rest of the species by having the set of the following cultural symbols/CS of the THD: language, thought, religion, knowledge/sciences, myths, cultural values and norms, etc. In the Quran terms, the THD has empowered humans to become most honored by God across all the species and given, thus, the privileged prestigious status of the *Khilafa*/vicarship on earth.

From the view of social sciences, the Quran's great emphasis on the high importance of the THD in human make-up is quite compatible with cultural sociology, a fast-growing branch of the current discipline of sociology. As mentioned, cultural sociology gives priority to the role of cultural factors in the understanding and explaining of both human individual and collective behaviors and the dynamics of societies, as American cultural sociologists and the author of this book are engaged to do, though within different perspectives.

The Symbolism Behind Advancing Hearing Over Seeing in the Quran

Having provided our genuine interpretation of the culturally credible reason behind the beginning of the Quranic revelations by the verb 'read', we find it appropriate to support our argument with another example from the text of the Quran. The latter uses the words of hearing and sight as nouns, adjectives, and verbs. The word *hearing* in its various forms comes systematically before the word *sight* in its different forms. There are 14 verses in the Quran that illustrate this order between the words of hearing and sight. Three examples are sufficient to make the point: 1—'Verily, We created Man from a drop of mingled sperm in order to try him: so We give him (the gift) of Hearing and Sight' (76:2). 2—'There is nothing like into Him, and He is the One That hears and sees' (42:11).3—'For Allah Who hears and sees (all things)'(31:28).

Advancing 14 times the word hearing in its various forms over the word sight in its various forms can hardly be just by chance but rather by a strong intention. It is common in different languages that authors advance words over other words to indicate their greater importance. As such, mentioning the word sight in its different forms 14 times following equally the mentioning of the word hearing in its various forms *shows clearly and with transparency* that hearing has more importance over sight.

Hearing as a Source of Human Culture

Hearing represents the unique way to fulfill the potential cultural features of humans referred to earlier. It is through hearing that humans can learn languages and consequently the THD. As stated before, language is *the Mother* of all cultural symbols. So, the great important function of hearing to humans comes from the fact it is the fundamental basis for the birth, development, and maturation of THD. As such, humans who are born deaf can hardly become great scholars, scientists, intellectuals, etc. while humans who are born blind or become blind at an early age can accomplish great achievements in the various cultural fields. Taha Hussein the late contemporary famous Egyptian intellectual is a telling example.

First Priority to Knowledge and Science

Based on the priority given to THD in the Islamic perspective, the thirst for knowledge and science is a hardcore religious value of Islam. As outlined, in the first revelation encounter between the Prophet and the Divine, top priority was not given to economics or material issues but rather to reading and the use of the pen as crucial tools/kits for the acquisition of knowledge and science. As underlined, social psychologists argue that first human impressions have a longer lifespan in human memories. So, the first divine revelation ought, therefore, to strongly draw Muhammad's attention to *the most important thing* that humans must acquire and master in this world and must not marginalize it, let alone forget it, to be truly God's vicar.

As such, from a social psychology outlook, the extreme divine emphasis and stress in the Quran on the acquisition of science and knowledge as a *first-class priority* for the good of humans has to be taken as fully intentional and not just an arbitrary thing in the first verse of the Quran. As a result, Muslim civilization has proven its remarkable achievement in knowledge and science in its golden age. The *Canon of Medicine of Avicenna* (980–1037) was the standard text in the medieval world including Europe. As to the Muslim philosopher Averroes (1126–98), his rational thinking is seen by many as the preview of the European Renaissance that came centuries later. Ibn Khaldun's sociological thought (1332–1406) in his *Muqaddimah* was over four centuries ahead of that of August Comte (1798–1857), the founding father of contemporary Western sociology. A Toynbee thinks very highly of Ibn Khaldun's articulate social science thought: "He has conceived and formulated a philosophy of history which is certainly the greatest work of its kind that has ever yet been created by any mind in any time and place" (Toynbee, 1956:322). Ibn Khaldun's great work in his *Muqaddimah* is the outcome of *Islamic epistemology and methodology* in the various fields of science and knowledge. That is, Muslim scientists and scholars use both reason and revelation in the creation as well as the acquisition of science and knowledge.

Here, there is an *intimate cooperation between the sacred and the mundane* in the field of science and knowledge. The Arabic two terms for that combination are Aql/reason and Naql/revelation. As such, our interpretation of the symbolic meaning of starting the Quran revelations with the verb 'read' falls within the framework of that Islamic epistemology and methodology.

Society and Culture as Means of Understanding and Explanation

In order to grasp the impact, the THD/culture has on people's behaviors in societies, there is a need for the approaches of social sciences to shed light on the concepts of *society* and *culture*. Sociologists and anthropologists use these two concepts as two hypothetical concepts to understand and explain human behaviors and social phenomena at large.

Social structure is defined by both sociologists and anthropologists as a basic permanent system of social roles and relations that make human groups organized in an interdependent manner that resembles that of the organs of living beings (*Encyclopedia of Sociology* 1974:70).

As to the anthropologist Bronislaw Malinowski and his followers, they have never accepted the hypothetical concept of social structure, but they have rather given greater importance to *cultural patterns*. It could be said that the hypotheses of differences between the two groups of sociologists and anthropologists are due to the differences between their disciplines. Anthropology focuses on the study of cultural aspects of society while sociology pays more attention to the social structure of society. This does not mean that the two perspectives entirely exclude each other's hypothesis: that of social structure or culture. So, sociologists and social anthropologists give priority to the study of the hypothesis of the social structure of society, and cultural anthropologists and cultural sociologists focus on the study of the culture hypothesis as *an independent variable* (Turner 2001:135–147).

Based on what has already been explored in the preceding pages of this chapter, the THD is very central to human identity. So, the analysis of this chapter gives *more credit* to the *cultural factors hypothesis* than to that of social structure, without eliminating altogether the impact of social structure's influence on people's behaviors. In other words, *no equal weight is given to the social and cultural factors* as two principal hypotheses in order to understand and explain a large number of phenomena in human communities and societies.

Social Determinism in Sociology

There is a full consensus among ancient and contemporary sociologists that social factors do have a great influence on people's behaviors. Ibn Khaldun speaks of man as a product of his social milieu. He believes that man's behaviors are the result of the social context in which he/she is being socialized. He expresses his genuine observation explicitly this way: "*Man is a child of the customs* and the things he/she has become *used to*. He/she is not the product of his natural disposition and temperament. The conditions to which he/she has become accustomed until they have become for him/her a quality of character and matters of habit and customs have replaced his/her natural disposition" (Dawood 1974:95).

Ibn Khaldun's perspective on human nature itself strongly emphasizes the importance of *social determinism* in which sociologists strongly believe throughout the ages. This may allow one to say that the expression 'man is, by nature, a social being' should have a new meaning that stipulates that man is first of all a being whose personality displays the social forces of the milieu where he/she is born and socialized.

It is hardly acceptable to raise the idea of social determinism in Western contemporary sociological thought without referring to Durkheim's thinking who had invented a new concept called 'les faits sociaux: social facts' (Durkheim 1981:5). He means by social facts the practiced living patterns of work, thinking and feeling ways which are completely independent of the will of individuals. Durkheim considers *social facts as overwhelming forces* as far as their influence on the behaviors of the individuals who finish by adopting and defending them wholeheartedly.

The Missing THD Input

As such, Ibn Khaldun and Durkheim are *social constructionists*. Yet, their descriptions of the role of social influences on the individuals' behaviors *do not explicitly mention* the reason which explains that: what makes Durkheim's social facts so imposing on individuals or what makes the social milieu's input able to replace innate dispositions among individuals as Ibn Khaldun states?

Unlike the claim of this chapter's thesis, neither Durkheim nor Ibn Khaldun refers with transparency to the hypothesis of *the prominent role of the cultural factors/the HTD*, which distinguishes the human race, as a crucial main factor that determines the important impact on people's behaviors in society. In this context, it may be genuine to blame more Durkheim than Ibn Khaldun as far as remaining silent on *the cultural influences* in the analysis of the nature of social influences (social facts) on the individuals' behaviors; since the present meaning of the concept of culture, as defined in contemporary social sciences, was hardly in existence when Ibn Khaldun wrote his famous work: *The Muqaddimah.*

The THD as a Dynamic Force of Influence on Behaviors

It can be said that Ibn Khaldun and Durkheim's views on the strong impact of social factors on people's behaviors can hardly be understood without taking into account implicitly or explicitly the hypothesis that *man is fully a human THD being* (Dhaouadi 2013:31–35). That is, the THD (spoken and written language, thought, religion, knowledge/science, myths, cultural values, and norms) is at *the center of the human identity* as shown repeatedly in previous chapters. Consequently, the absence or the marginality of the hypothesis of the centrality of THD in man's identity makes it difficult to analyze the overpowering influence of social factors on the behaviors of individuals. In other words, it makes the claimed strong impact of social forces on behaviors and social phenomena rather *mechanical* disregarding the potential impact of cultural factors/the THD at least as *an intervening variable*. It may be strongly legitimate to state that *humans* are in fact *symbolic/cultural beings* before being social in both Khaldunian and Durkheimian senses. The claim of the THD hypothesis derives from the previously made argument in this chapter and earlier ones, based on the five observations of five distinct human features that enable the human species to be the single dominant race over the rest of the species (see the Drawing above).

Cultural Psychology and Sociology and the THD

The THD thesis in this chapter is strongly in line with the emergence and rapid growth and development of two social science disciplines:

cultural psychology and cultural sociology. The former assumes the idea that *culture and mind are inseparable*. Richard Shweder, one of the major proponents of the field of cross-cultural psychology, defines this new discipline as the study of psychological and behavioral tendencies as human features rooted in and embodied in culture (Shweder 1999:10). As to cultural sociology, it is growing field in its own especially in the USA as stated at the outset of this chapter by one of its leading figures: "over the past ten to fifteen years, 'culture' has developed to become one of the most popular and important areas within sociology in the United States" (Smith 1998:1).

THD Marginalization in Theorizing on the Individual and Society

Despite the ongoing increasing interest in the study of culture in many disciplines, the idea of this chapter concerning *the centrality* of the THD in man and society's identity is not yet a prominent feature in contemporary social sciences. There is rather a marginalization of the importance of culture and its central and decisive role in helping to understand and explain human phenomena. This marginalization would *damage* the credibility of these sciences. Giddens' structuration theory and Bourdieu's concept of 'habitus' hardly make reference to the THD as the core for the making of structuration and the habitus (Giddens, Sutton 2014:25). One may describe the thought of these social sciences as a thought which has given a priori attention to what is close to the important (economic, political, social) instead of giving their focusing attention to *the most important dimensions in man and society's represented by the THD/culture* (Dhaouadi 2006 b:28).

The social sciences' marginalization of the appropriate impact of culture on the shaping of individual and collective behaviors is likely to be the outcome of three major factors:

1. The definitions of the term 'culture' itself: The meaning of the term has been highly contested especially within anthropology

from Tylor's to those of late anthropologists like Kroeber, Kluckhohn, Mead, and Boas. These anthropologists have focused on the *external side of culture/ the THD* and hardly on the inside one. That is, they have focused on both artifacts and behaviors. For Herskovits "Culture is the man-made part of the environment." As to Mead, culture "is the total shared, learned behavior of a society or a sub-group." Malinowski's formulation of culture describes also the external dimensions of culture: "Culture is a well-organized unity divided into two fundamental aspects—a body of artifacts and a system of customs" (White 1973:32–34). Bidney would attribute the classification of the above conceptualization of culture to what he calls 'the realistic' approach (Kinkaid 2012:393).

2. There are in such definitions of culture *two missing things*: a) What is the origin of culture or where it comes from? Why other living species do not have a culture like the human one though they have bodies and live in the environment? b) There is negligence to the substance of the nature of the symbolic/non-material side of human culture as represented in the concept/theory of the THD.

3. All the above definitions of culture by anthropologists *fail to speak of the THD* as having *no weight and no volume* in the material sense of the words as the THD paradigm emphasizes. This vision of the THD permits to see them as having what we call *transcendental features* as shown in the following example:

   The THD has *neither weight nor volume* in the material sense of the word. That is, the THD does not have a material nature, but it has a rather non-material/ transcendental/spiritual nature. Positivist social scientists are very likely to find it strange to use the terms 'weight and volume' in dealing with the THD/culture. Nonetheless, neutral objectivity strongly permits the usage of such terms and will give a lot of meaning to this kind of use. It may be sufficient to mention in this context a few examples to make the point:

I.   Why do letters and documents sent by fax and e-mail reach their destination much faster than if they were mailed by regular or even rapid/fast mail? The explanation for this, through the concept of weightless and no volume, could be simply put this way: the process of sending letters and documents by e-mail and fax *eliminates* from them the factors of *material weight and volume*.

II.   With the absolute intrinsic absence of weight and volume in the natural essence of the THD system, it becomes quite appropriate to understand why the THD components can move with high and unbelievable speed through time and space.

III.   The THD having no material weight and volume may help also explain how it is possible to put the enormous written material of tons of books in a few small electronic flash disks whose weight and volume are too little. This is possible because the words of the books (in this case) having by their very nature no volume and weight *hardly need huge material space* to be contained in it. In philosophical and religious senses, the THD belongs to the spiritual and non-material world of humans. The THD has its own special characteristics and laws by which they abide and ultimately make them different from the world which has both weight and volume.

IV.   The extremely rapid speed of sound is another example which is frequently cited. The Concorde plane's fast speed is often compared to that of the sound. This could be explained by the fact that the transmitted word, through the voice-sound at a short distance between individuals or at a far distance during their phone calls, has at its natural state neither weight nor volume. Consequently, the voiced-sent word is naturally predisposed to move with extreme speed.

V.   The THD has a *longer lifespan* throughout time. Ideas, religious beliefs, cultural values, and norms have a long lifespan potential of survival which may last for semi-eternity. Written and spoken languages play fundamental roles in the very making of the THD and its longer lifespan survival. This is because language is considered by us in this book as *the Mother of all elements of the THD,* as stated several times in the chapters of this book. That is to say, the THD/culture system can hardly exist without the presence of the human language in its spoken form at least. As such, one can argue that human language has a potential *eternalizing mark/seal* which influences all components of the THD.

This present new outlook on the long lifespan of the THD helps explain the phenomena of the so-called *eternal and semi-eternal human thought* of philosophers, scientists, scholars, and religious thinkers of various civilizations since time immemorial. Their thought potential eternity can be accounted for, first, by the use of spoken and written languages which have the eternalizing seal as just mentioned and, second, by the fact that *human thought belongs to the transcendental universe of the THD.*

The Rational Choice Theory

The THD perspective presented in the previous pages is different from what is called Rational Choice Theory in today's social sciences. Smith states that this theory *rejects culture* altogether by looking at society as made up of rational selfish actors who attempt always to maximize the profit in their social actions (Smith 1998:3). Thus, the behaviors of the individuals in society are but the total sum of the individual behaviors. The latter are always the outcome of a personal desire (rational) which is influenced first of all by the powerful force of a strong commitment to achieve most of his/her personal benefits and interests. The thesis of the Rational Choice Theory is *in opposition* to Ibn Khaldun and contemporary sociology's views as well as of the THD regarding their influence on people's behaviors as already explained. Ibn Khaldun has given great importance to two social factors which strongly determine the behaviors of individuals and groups and the dynamics of human societies. Al Assabiyya (group feeling) and religion are very influential social factors in Arab Muslim societies. Contemporary sociologists have stressed the influence of several forces like the income and culture of social classes on the behaviors of the individuals and groups in human societies and civilizations (Dortier 2004:703). Furthermore, the focus in this book on the THD influences on people's behaviors obviously *does not agree* with the thesis of the Rational Choice Theory.

The Principles of the Rational Choice Theory

Since 1999, two important academic studies have been published on the Rational Choice Theory. The first appeared in 1999 in the Journal of *Current Sociology* as a report on this theory (Zafirovski 1999:47–132). As to the second study, it was published as a chapter (chapter III) in *the International Handbook of Sociology* (Quah, Sales 2000:50–83). The author of the first study and the two authors of chapter III present *the main ideas* of the Rational Choice Theory which *rejects culture* as an important factor for human behavior. The first one summarizes the ideas of this theory as follows: In sociology, the Rational Choice Theory seeks to help rationalize the concept of the impact of the rational beneficial economic input on people's behaviors. That is, individuals have the tendency to seek the maximum benefits through their continuing calculation of *the equation of losses and gains*. For better precision, the proponents of the Rational Choice Theory define rationality as the achievement of the maximum of things by reducing the losses to their extreme minimum level and increasing the gains to their extreme maximum level (Zafirouvski 1999:47). On the other hand, the authors of chapter III of the Handbook emphasize that David Hume and Adam Smith were pioneers of the Rational Choice Theory. These two English social thinkers believed in the existence of one *universal human nature* whose main characteristics are the following: people's behaviors are the outcome of their desire to achieve their interests in personal goals (Turner 2001:51). But Hume and Smith and others point out that *people do not always act in a narrow way that serves only their interests.* As to the other principle of the framework of the Rational Choice Theory, it is represented by the behaviors of learning: people who respond positively in a repeated manner to the environment that gives them rewards. Usually, people choose those behaviors associated with positive stimuli (Turner 2001:51).

The Rational Choice Theory in Question

A lot of criticism was addressed to the Rational Choice Theory. It is criticized because it considers *human beings as simple rational ones*, in the sense they always seek to attain the maximum profit and the minimum loss in their behaviors in order to fulfill their personal interests and goals. So, the critics believe it is appropriate to take into consideration the influential factors of the *cultural system* and the social milieu on people's behaviors as does the THD perspective in this book. Those factors constitute the main strong forces that can orient human behaviors (Dortier 2004:705, Green, Shapiro 1994:105). This attitude supports both perspectives of Ibn Khaldun and contemporary sociology and this chapter's view as well as the perspectives of the other chapters. Here are some of Zafirovski's telling reservations toward the Rational Choice Theory:

1. There is a big paradox in the thesis of this theory. While the utilitarian approach (gain and loss) lacks credibility even in the explanation of economic phenomena. Yet, it is being exported

to other branches of social sciences which study non-economic phenomena.

2. The application of this theory in all social sciences makes the non-economic phenomena, as social structures and cultural patterns, look like the outcome of the relation among the individuals seeking for themselves the maximum benefits in their interaction with others. While the opposite view offers a better explanation. That is, cultural patterns and social structures create in society the basic personality of individuals who would always seek profit and avoid loss in social interactions (Zafirovski 1999:102–103).

3. A large number of sociologists in Europe and the USA tend to use the Rational Choice Theory (Quah, Sales 2000:50). However, the two authors of this Handbook of sociology underline what they call '*anomalies*' of this theory through empirical testing. In doing so, *the findings contradict the predictions of this theory* (Quah, Sales, 2000:50).

The Rational Choice Theory and Behavior

It is clear by now that the nature of the leading causes of the prevailing human behavior in society differs between the Rational Choice Theory and the impact of THD on human behaviors. On the one hand, the Rational Choice Theory almost sees *humans as economic beings by nature* seeking permanent profit and avoiding loss in all human behaviors. That is, this economic behavior looks like a well-rooted innate one in human nature across the ages among humans in all societies and civilizations. On the other hand, the THD paradigm emphasizes that behaviors in human societies are the outcome of influential cultural factors (cultural constructionism). If the tendency to always seek profit and avoid loss is deeply rooted in human nature, humans would have been *identical* in this regard in all places and at all times. For instance, the big existing differences in profit and loss-oriented behaviors between capitalist Western societies and many other contemporary societies are *related to powerful socio-cultural factors and not to general factors in human nature* as claimed by the Rational Choice Theory. This can be summarized in contemporary Western societies in two examples:

1- As mentioned before, Adam Smith's time in the eighteenth century (1723–1790) was associated with the call for Liberalism and Individualism.

2- The contemporary capitalist system especially in American society has greatly influenced the process of socialization of Western individuals in a way that gives priority to the values of material individual gains and at the same time it abhors also the idea of loss. The outcome of *this global socio-cultural socialization* of the individuals, the communities, and the social classes in Western contemporary societies has led to the making of a general Western basic personality whose behavior has *a semi-full influence culturally and socially on people's behaviors* in those societies. For instance, Americans have collectively the tendency that everyone pays his/her coke, coffee, and tea when they go together to McDonald's, a cafeteria, or a restaurant. It is called in the USA: 'GoDutch'. This is the prevailing cultural norm among the members of the American society. The opposite of this behavior can be found in societies much poorer than American society. That is, individuals like to pay for the drinks of their friends and colleagues. In fact, some of these individuals believe it is almost a scandal to see everyone pay for his/her drinks. In both examples, the prevailing *cultural norm* in favor of the principle 'everyone pays his/her own' or 'one person pays for the drinks of friends/colleagues' is a behavior in which various socio-cultural factors have helped its emergence and its wide or full total spread in society.

Cultural Socialization

This chapter's thesis on the centrality of THD in human identity *helps* us understand and explain how human behaviors are strongly shaped by cultural factors/the THD. These behaviors are the outcome of what sociologists call *socialization.* The latter is but a process by which the individual learns the patterns of social life and assimilates them to become ultimately the basis of the making of his/her social personality. Human socialization is a complex and long process that can hardly have an end before death. The role of the THD in the making of human socialization hardly needs elaboration. It is through the spoken, written, and sign languages in the social milieu that humans learn religious beliefs, cultural values, norms, myths, rituals, systems of knowledge, and science. The full success of socialization among the members of a given society makes the socialization heritage *a deeply rooted reality* in the core of the basic personality of those individuals or a social habit that resembles innate things in the human personality, as Ibn Khaldun had pointed out earlier in this chapter.

In other words, the behaviors of the majority of people become something automatic or semi-automatic as a result of what the individuals have learned through the system of the THD from the socio-cultural heritage of their societies. Based on this, we believe it is *more accurate* to change the term socialization to become *cultural socialization* because of the crucial importance of the THD in the socialization process. So, the THD is *the Mother source* for the making of the various patterns of collective behaviors in human groups, societies, and civilizations.

This new concept of *cultural socialization* is the outcome of the core of this chapter's epistemological view of the THD/culture presented in this chapter and most of the other chapters in this book. Etymologically, the concept of socialization appears to stress most the impact of society (structural explanation) (Alexander, Jacobs, Smith 2012:6–7) in shaping the individual's personality and behavior, thus, neglecting the influence of the role of culture/ THD in this process.

Conclusion

This chapter can be considered to have genuinely met its task to underline *two new features*:

1. The formulation of the THD theory/paradigm through *the five first-hand observations* is something rather new. Contemporary anthropologists and sociologists have written a lot theoretically and empirically about culture. To our modest knowledge, the basis on which they have established their cultural theory is different from *the thesis presented in this chapter and in the entire book*. For instance, while the emergence of cultural sociology is seen by its proponents as the result of rebellion against Parsons (Alexander, Jacobs, Smith 2012:6–7), we look at it in this chapter and elsewhere as the outcome of the assumptions that humans are by nature cultural beings (Dhaouadi 2013:79).

2. The emphasis on the cultural roots/ THD of behaviors makes the author of this chapter inclined to modify the concept of socialization to become more accurate and transparent in its definition of the term socialization. As such, it has become preferable to use the new term *cultural socialization* instead of the single term socialization which is widely used in modern social sciences. Cultural socialization, as a new concept, strongly stresses the major important role that the THD plays in the socialization process.

References

Alatas, F. (2006) *Alternative Discourses in Asian Social Science: Responses to Eurocentrism,* New Delhi, ThousandOaks, London, Sage Publication.

Alexander, J. et al. (2012) *The Oxford Handbook of Cultural Sociology,* Oxford, Oxford University Press.

Calhoun, C. (ed.2007) *Sociology in America,* Chicago, the University of Chicago Press.

Compiègne, I. (2011) *La société numérique en question,* Auxerre Cedex: Editions Sciences Humaines.

Dawood, N. J. (ed.1974*) Ibn Khaldun: The Muqaddimah: An Introduction to History,* New Jersey, Princeton University Press.

Dhaouadi, M. (2013) *Cultural Sociology within Innovative Treatise: Islamic Insights on Human Symbols,* Lanham, New York, London, University Press of America, Inc.

Dhaouadi, M. (2013c) 'Humanity as Homo Culturus,*'American Journal of Islamic Social Sciences,*30, 2, 77–102.

Dhaouadi, M. (2006a) *Culture in Islamic and Social Science Perspectives* (in Arabic) Beirut, Dar AlkitabAljadid LTD.

Dhaouadi, M. (2006b) *The Other Face of Tunisian Modern Society* (in Arabic) Tunis, L'Or du Temps.

Dortier, J.-F. (2004) *Le dictionnaire des sciences humaines,* Auxerre Cedex, Editions Sciences Humaines.

Durkheim, E. (1981) *Les règles de la méthode sociologique*, Paris, Quadrige/PUF.

Encyclopedia of Sociology (1974), Guilford/USA, the Dushkin Publishing Group, Inc.
Giddens, A & Sutton, Ph. (2014) *Essential Concepts in Sociology*, Cambridge, Polity Press.

Green, D., Shapiro, I. (1994) *Pathologies of Rational Choice Theory: A Critique of Applications in Political Science*, New Haven, Yale University Press.

Kincaid, H. (2012) *The Oxford Handbook of Philosophy of Social Science*, Oxford, Oxford University Press.

Quah, R. Stella, Sales, Arnaud (2000) *The International Handbook of Sociology*, London, Sage Publications.

Science et Avenir Magazine, Jan–Feb 2012.

Semashko, L., and others (2006) *International Sociology Review of Books*, 2, 6,829–38.

Shweder, R. (1999) *Cultural Psychology: Essays on Comparative Human Development*, Cambridge, Cambridge University Press.

Smith, Ph. (1998) *The New American Cultural Sociology*, Cambridge, Cambridge University Press.

Spillman, L, ed. (2007) *Cultural Sociology*, Malden, Blackwell Publishing.

Tuner, J-H (ed.2001) *Handbook of Sociological Theory,* New York, Kluwer Academic/Plenum Publishers.

Wieviorka, M. (2007) *Les sciences sociales en mutation,* Auxerrescedex, Editions Sciences Humaines.

White, l. (1973) *The Concept of Culture,* Edina, MN, Alpha Editions.

Wolff, j. (September 1999) 'Cultural Studies and the Sociology of Culture,'*Contemporary Sociology,* 28,5,499–506.

Zafirovski, M. (1999) 'What is Really Rational Choice? Beyond the Utilitarian Concept of Rationality,' *Current Sociology.*

Chapter VI
The Arab World Dialogue with the West: Within the Third Human Dimension Outlook

Introduction

This chapter proposes *a different perspective* to look at the potential dialogue between the Arab World and the West. This perspective is one of the outcomes of our continuing research in the field of human cultural symbols/ THD on which we have been doing the so-called *Basic Research* for over four decades as expressed in previous chapters. The focus of this type of research has led us, among other things, to invent a new terminology for the study of what is human culture in society. As emphasized in those chapters, we use the THD instead of human cultural symbols in the analysis of cultural aspects in human societies.

Dialogue Between the Arab World and the West

Based on the assumptions of our concept/paradigm of the THD, we would like to argue in this chapter that *the West is less predisposed* than the Arab World for civilization dialogue (Dhaouadi 2005:8–15). Consequently, the West may be considered as the major source of Huntington's so-called Clash of Civilizations. Our observation is largely different from Huntington's set of ideas (Huntington 1993). Our main thesis here is based on the assumptions that *common cultures* (languages, religious beliefs, cultural values...) among peoples, societies and nations are *essential factors* that encourage and facilitate contacts and dialogues between societies of different civilizations belongings. Conversely, the lack or the absence of common cultures between humans would discourage and hamper contacts and dialogues and, subsequently, create conditions that may favor tensions, clashes, and conflicts among them. We will explain in this chapter how *the widespread knowledge* of Western languages, Christian beliefs, and Western knowledge-science and cultural values system (THD) among the large population of the Arab World incite Arabs to desire to have contact and dialogue with Westerners and their civilization.

Our THD Theory

The above thesis on the importance of these shared THD elements for civilizations' dialogue is based on our own basic research observations and findings. As already outlined, the latter have made us strongly claim that *"humans are by nature cultural symbolic beings."* That is, cultures represent the core of the identities of human individuals and their societies and civilizations. We came to this conclusion as a result of the following explanations and arguments.

As underlined repeatedly, the THD is all those distinctive human symbolic traits: spoken and written language, thought, religion, knowledge/science, myths, laws, cultural values, and norms. Our analysis of the THD system had made us realize that language is the Mother of all components of the THD, as mentioned frequently. This means that none of the remaining elements of the THD can really exist without the prior existence of human language in its spoken form at least. In other words, *human language is the single most important source for the emergence of the phenomenon of human culture/ THD* (Dhaouadi 2006). This observation on the fundamental extreme importance of language in the making of human culture is hardly made manifest by today's social scientists in the East and the West.

Our above claim that THD/culture is at the very center of human identity is based on a number of our own observations with regard to *five features* that strongly distinguish the human race from the other species. To our knowledge, both the identification and the use of the five features in question are entirely *new* in dealing with the centrality of culture for the human species. For instance, modern anthropological and sociological works and that of Edward Said on culture are not similar to our own in their methodology as well as in their assumptions (White 1973, Said 1993). As stressed before, let's take a close look now at the novelty of the study of the human five distinct features leading to the central role of culture in the making of human identity:

1. The process of the human body's growth and maturation is *very slow* in comparison with those of other living beings.
2. In general, humans have a *longer lifespan* than those of most of the other species as shown in one of the chapters of this book.
3. The human race is radically distinguished from the other species by its *dominant role* in the management of this world.
4. Humans are decisively privileged from the other living species by the THD.
5. Based on the nature of the THD, the human identity is made up of three parts: the body, the soul, and the THD. Thus, it is fully a *tri-dimensional identity*.

Then, the appropriate question that ought to be raised now is the following: Are there *relationships* between those five distinct human features?

There is certainly a direct relation between 1 and 2. Because the slow human body growth and maturation necessarily requires a longer lifespan to enable the full realization of the different and diverse phases of bio-physiological growth and maturation. Consequently, the link between 1 and 2 is of *causal nature*. Unfortunately, neither *Scientific American* (SA) Magazine nor the *New Scientist* have provided me with solid scientific data that explain the factors behind the slowness of the human body's growth and maturation. SA has just advised me (October

19, 2005) to do the following "you might try searching anthropology websites for possible answers."

As to the bi-dimensional human identity, it is also *a direct outcome* of the human body and the THD.

The search for a relationship between man's domination factor and his remaining four distinct features strongly shows that features 1 and 2 hardly predispose man to be the unique dominant being over the other species in this planet. Since humans are, for example, much weaker physically than many other species. As such, it could implicitly be hypothesized and suggested that man's dominant role is strongly related to features 5 and 4, already underlined: The human dualistic identity (body and THD) where THD is shared by both. Thus, THD appears to be *the masterpiece of human identity.*

THD's principal role in the determination of human destiny goes even further than just the central place that man occupies in the world. The importance of THD manifests also itself indirectly in features 1 and 2. *The slow human body growth and maturation* could hypothetically be explained by the fact that human global growth and maturation involve *two fronts*: The body front as well as that of THD.

In contrast, the body growth and maturation of the rest of the species are overall of *rapid nature*, because it is assumed that it is due to the absence of THD in the non-human species. In short, while the growth and maturation of non-human species are *uni-dimensional*: the body and their human counterparts are *bi-dimensional* (the body and THD). That is, human growth and maturation involve two fronts: the cultural symbolic dimension as well as the human body dimension. Thus, the rapidity or the slow pace of the entire growth and maturation processes of the species depends on the variable/factor of the uni-dimensionality or the bi-dimensionality of growth and maturation of the entities of living species. The following drawing shows THD centrality in the human entity. This loudly supports the strong legitimacy of my own theory which advocates that, *"Man is by nature a cultural symbolic being."*

Drawing

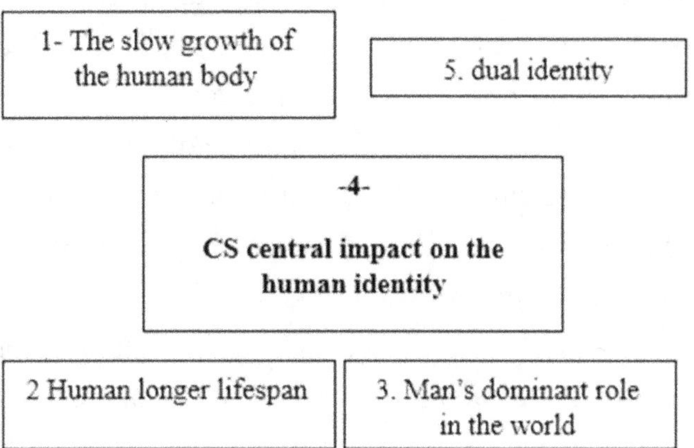

The above drawing clearly shows that *CS/ THD is very central to human identity*. This grants credit to my claim here and elsewhere (Dhaouadi 2002, 2008) that THD has indeed *a global effect on human destiny and affairs*. That is, humans are fundamentally cultural symbolic beings. As such, THD is the first direct and indirect strategic key that social scientists have at their disposal to understand and explain human behavior both in its individualistic and collective sense.

THD and Cultural Dialogue

Having just repeated our thesis of THD because it is very suitable for this chapter's main argument. As such, the THD theory helps put the issue of civilizations dialogue or clash into perspective. First, based on the centrality of THD in the human identity it is more appropriate to use the term *culture* instead of civilization in the analysis of the issue of dialogue between today's peoples, societies, and civilizations. This is, because *culture* is, on the one hand, *the basic founding element of a given civilization* and, on the other hand, it is the decisive force in determining and encouraging the dialogue process or vice versa between humans. So, it is more accurate to speak of *cultural dialogue* rather than civilizations dialogues.

Since the end of the twentieth century, many books and articles have been published on this subject as well as numerous seminars, colloquiums, and congresses have been held in different parts of the world. The success of the project of civilizations dialogue could hardly crystallize and be fruitful without the dialogue of the cultures of human civilizations. Because cultures/ THD represents the core of the identities of human individuals and their societies and civilizations, as stressed above in the argument of my own THD theory.

Given that languages are, according to the assumptions of the THD theory, the essential creating forces of the phenomenon of human cultures, it becomes very appropriate to consider *peoples' learning of each other languages* as a practical and effective *green visa* that facilitates the process of dialogue between the concerned parties whose civilizations have a wish to dialogue. (Bochner 1985:99–126)

However, today Western, advanced societies and developing countries are *not equal* on the learning scale of each other languages. At least some large social groups from the South know fairly well some of the languages of the Western developed countries. English and French are the most widely known and used Western languages in the Third World. All social groups and classes of Western advanced societies *do not have* even a limited knowledge of the Third World's languages.

This situation is true of the state of dialogue between the Western world and the Arab World. Calls in favor of such a dialogue have been getting stronger, especially since September 11, 2001. From the point of view of my CS/ THD theory, *the West is less ready and skilled linguistically and, thus, culturally* to get into a serious and wide dialogue with the Arab World. For that matter, all Western social classes do not know any of the major languages of the Arab Muslim world which are: Arabic, Persian, Turkish, and Urdu. This situation leads, consequently, to the *widespread Western ignorance of the cultures of the Arab Muslim societies.* (Bochner 1985:5–4, 81–98). This could hardly encourage and enable the West for a wide grass root of Arab Muslim languages and cultures.

Dialogue with the Arab World.

In this regard, *Americans* may be considered—in linguistic and cultural terms—less predisposed to dialogue with other cultures. They may be so because they are *more handicapped* by their wide ignorance of foreign languages than most of the advanced European Western societies. In my own terms, they are massively illiterate of foreign language(s) as *green visa tool* that could solicit them to enter into dialogue with others. This may be one of the reasons that helps explain why *the slogan of Clash of Civilizations* has come from the *US culture* and not from the European one.

In contrast to that, there is in the Arab societies a wide genuine knowledge of Western cultures because of the widespread usage, particularly of English and French in those societies during Western colonization and after especially among the elites and the middle and the higher classes of the Arab population. As such, my CS/ THD theory shows that the desire for civilization dialogue *is not equal* between the Western advanced societies and the Arab peoples. The greater knowledge of Western languages and cultures among the Arab population enables them to have greater motivation and aspiration than their Western counterparts to strongly welcome and act in favor of the dialogue with the West.

The Arab World *scores also better* than the West on the *religious scale of knowledge*. On the one hand, Muslims strongly believe in Moses and Jesus as prophets and God's messengers. The belief in other divine prophets and messengers throughout the ages is a fundamental component of the Muslim faith. Consequently, Christians and Jews are seen by Muslims as the Peoples of the Revealed Books.

On their part, Judaism and Christianity do not preach to their followers to believe in Islam and Mohammad as its prophet and messenger.

In other words, the West shows great ignorance of the Arab Muslim world's languages, religions, and cultures. As already mentioned, social psychologists would strongly point out that ignorance of other people's cultures constitutes a major source for *the display of prejudices, stereotyped attitudes,* and *widespread false accusations of them* (Bochner 1985:5–44).

Furthermore, the West remains today the dominant power in this world. Certainly, these two sets of factors have the tendency *to reinforce* each other in order to establish an inferior image of Arabs and Muslims and at the same time a superior image of Westerners.

According to the CS/ THD theory, the population of the Western world at large has *more difficulty linguistically and religiously* than its Arab and Muslim counterparts to really engage in *a fair grass roots dialogue*. As such, the West is far from being adequately prepared to advocate, in a spontaneous and motivated manner, an open and sincere dialogue with the Arab and Muslim world with all respect and equality.

Huntington's thesis does not make mention of the importance of the presence or the absence of linguistic and religious factors in the making of dialogue or Clash of Civilizations. As shown, these factors point out that the Arab Muslim world has a greater desire and willingness to engage in dialogue with the Western world.

Furthermore, Huntington's theoretical assumptions display a lot of prejudice and misunderstanding not only toward the Arab Muslim civilization but toward the Chinese civilization as well. Such an attitude does not surely help the establishment of credible scientific knowledge and science. Huntington's view lacks the full presence of a neutral and objective spirit in advancing his theory of the Clash of Civilizations. Consequently, he cannot easily claim to be one of those who really have committed themselves to science as *their true vocation*.

Western Sciences Appeal Opens Dialogue with the West

In addition to the already mentioned factors inviting Arabs and Muslims alike to welcome dialogue with the Western world, there is also the factor of the West's great advancement and leadership in modern science and knowledge that strongly encourages the Arabs and Muslims to stress the major importance of opening the dialogue gate quite wide with the West. This is not only for pragmatic and beneficial reasons, as the case may be in many developing countries, but this is due as well to *the similarity between Islam and the West in their cultural value systems* which consider the promotion of knowledge and science as very central and a *first priority* in human societies and civilizations. This type of similarity does not only strengthen the desire for dialogue with the West among the Arabs and Muslims, but it may also solicit *Western respect* for the Arabs and Muslims who were pioneers in the development of science and knowledge which is seen by many as the basis for the rise of the European Renaissance. President Barack Obama's speech to the Muslim world from Cairo University on June 4, 2009, put into perspective Arab Muslim civilization's great contribution to the world heritage in science and knowledge.

The common praise of knowledge and science by both Islamic and Western cultures will be briefly described later on. With those underlined numerous positive factors in favor particularly of Arab Muslim dialogue and not Clash with the Western world, Huntington's theory of the Clash of Civilizations *needs to be questioned* in its crude application to the Arab Muslim world. The latter, as explained, has *many more strong reasons* than the West in favor of *dialoguing and not clashing* with the West.

Huntington's Theory in Question

Today, as already shown, there is an internationally wide use of the theory of the *Clash of Civilizations* in the media, in intellectual circles, and even in the common daily life of men and women around the world.

The events of September 11, 2001, may have boosted the popularity of this theory particularly in the United States.

The debate on the credibility of Huntington's theory is still waging out of which *two main camps* could be identified. On the one hand, one camp strongly believes in the importance of the theory especially for the understanding of the West's relation with the Arab Muslim world. On the other hand, the second camp seriously questions the very credibility of Huntington's theory. It is argued, for instance, that the idea of the Clash of Civilizations is the outcome of a *political situation*. It is an attempt to create a new paradigm that replaces the theory of the Cold War between the former Soviet Union and the Western world led by the USA. As such, the thesis of the theory of the Clash of Civilizations can hardly be considered a scientific one. Furthermore, there are those who see Huntington's theory as having a *philosophical background* related to the thinking of Thomas Kuhn, Oswald Spengler, Arnold Toynbee, and Fernand Braudel. This background may have overstretched the application of the assumptions of this theory to the Arab Muslim civilization whose many present parameters oppose the clash with Western civilization, as already pointed out in this chapter(Saadi 2006: 147–161).

The Islamic East and the Christian West Could Dialogue

In order to complete the assessment of the status of Huntington's theory and reduce its general confusing dimensions, I think it is appropriate now to take a closer look at *the similarity factor* in knowledge-science cultural value systems of both Arab Muslim and Western civilizations mentioned before in order to see how *dialogue with the West is heavily asked for* by today Arab Muslims because of the multiple factors at work explained here. This is clearly different from the claim of Huntington's theory of the Clash of Civilizations. This similarity factor in knowledge-science cultural values systems of Islam and the West is *hardly mentioned* let alone analyzed and discussed in studies of dialogue or clash of civilizations.

I examine here the attitude of both Arab Muslim and Western civilizations with regard to *one single important issue* for human civilization's progress and dynamics. This should greatly allow a decent evaluation of the degrees of *clashes or convergences* between these two civilizations. The theme on which to measure the stand of both civilizations is *the place* of *knowledge and science in their cultural value systems*.

There is overwhelming evidence that the acquisition of science and knowledge constitutes a central cultural value of modern Western civilization. That explains the West's leadership today in the tremendous science and knowledge explosion. The West's domination of the world scene is not, thus, limited to military and economic matters but it must be extended well beyond that to *its superiority* in the fields of knowledge and science which are certainly more strategic, in the long run, for the West's continuing domination of the world.

The origins of the West's leadership in these fields began with the clashes between the Church and the scientists in the late Middle Ages in Europe. With the victory of the latter came the Renaissance which strongly pushed forward the cultivation of secular knowledge and science that has since become the guiding ethics of contemporary Western civilization. With the passing of many centuries with science and knowledge experiences and the countless discoveries in natural and social sciences; has developed a general *attitude of highly praising learning and education* among the populations of advanced Western societies to the extent that a sort of sense of curiosity to explore practically everything in the world has become a widespread attitude among the citizens of those societies. So, the whole world/universe is an open vista for the Western mind.

The thirst for knowledge and science is also a fundamental feature of Arab Muslim civilization. The roots of that are, however, the very opposite of Western civilization's. They are to be traced to the original essence of the Islamic faith itself. The search for knowledge and science is *a hardcore religious value of Islam.* The very first words and verses revealed to the prophet Muhammad in the Quran leave no doubt about that: '*Read* in the name of your Lord and Cherisher…He Who taught the use of the Pen, taught man that he did not know' (S:96, v:1,4,5). In this first revelation encounter between the Prophet and the Divine, top priority was not given to economics or material issues but rather to reading and the use of the pen as crucial tools/kits for the acquisition of knowledge and science. Modern social psychology's insights greatly help us understand why *reading and the use of the pen* had to be mentioned to the Prophet before anything else. Social psychologists argue that *first human impressions have a longer lifespan in human memories.* So, the first divine revelation ought, therefore, *to strongly draw the prophet Muhammad's attention to the most important thing* that humans must acquire and master in this world and must not marginalize it, let alone forget it, to be truly God's vicar. As such, from a social psychology outlook, the extreme divine emphasis and stress in the Quran on the acquisition of science and knowledge as *a first-class priority* for the good of humans has to be taken as fully intentional and not just an arbitrary thing in the first verse of the Quran.

The stand of the two first references of Islam, the Quran and the Hadith (the Prophet's sayings and behavior), on the crucial importance of knowledge and science is so strong and breathtaking. It is estimated that about one-sixth (1/6) of the Quran's verses are directly or indirectly about science and knowledge and their *capital role* in the improvement of the human condition and destiny. The text of the Quran uses the word science to mean both knowledge and science. It uses the derivatives of the latter as well as an adjective and as a verb in the hundreds of its verses related to knowledge and science: "Are people who have knowledge/science equal to those who do not have them? Only true scholars/scientists revere God most."

The sayings of the Prophet are in turn in full support of knowledge and science as first-class cultural values of the Islamic religion:

"Seeking knowledge and science is a religious duty for every Muslim man and woman," "seek knowledge and science from the cradle to the grave," "seek knowledge and science as far as China," "scientists and scholars are the true inheritors of the prophets" (Sardar1984:18). The capital importance of science and knowledge is, therefore, extremely central in the cultural value system of the Islamic faith as fully expressed in these limited verses of the Quran and Hadiths. Thus, there is hardly any surprise for the milestones achieved in knowledge and science by Muslim civilization in its golden age. The *Canon of Medicine of Avicenna* (980–1037) was the standard text in the medieval world including Europe. As to the Muslim philosopher Averroes (1126–98), his rational thinking is seen by many as the preview of the European Renaissance that came centuries later. Ibn Khaldun's sociological thought (1332–1406) in his *Muqaddimah* was over four centuries ahead of that of August Comte (1798–1857), the founder of contemporary Western sociology. It surpasses Comte's on many levels by the admission of highly credible Western thinkers like the great British contemporary historian Arnold Toynbee who wrote of Ibn Khaldun: "He has conceived and formulated a philosophy of history which is certainly the greatest work of its kind that has ever yet been created by any mind in any time and place" (Toynbee 1956:372).

This *strong convergence* between these two civilizations on the high importance of knowledge and science should legitimately discredit the often taken-for-granted stand of the theory of the 'Clash of Civilizations'. The Muslim and Western civilizations have clearly *a solid common basis for rapprochement and solidarity*. What is certain in this regard is that Arabs and Muslims are today *strongly attracted* by Western civilization because of its command and lead in all fields of modern knowledge and science. This factor is extremely important for today's Arabs and Muslims *to promote the spirit of dialogue with the West and not clash with it.*

The Politics of Conflicts and Tensions between the West and Islam

In modern times, the tensions between them are largely of *political nature*. Huntington himself has referred to this: "…however, the age of Muslim wars has its roots in more general causes. These do not include the inherent nature of Islamic doctrine and beliefs…The causes of contemporary Muslim wars lie in politics, not in seventh-century religious doctrines." (Newsweek, 2001–2002:9)

There is no question today that the Arab and Muslim world's hostility toward the United States is strongly caused first in this century by the Bush administration's often unconditional support for Israel against the Palestinians. All signs could make one easily predict that the relations between the Arab and Muslim population and the US will take *a positive radical change* if the United States and the West, in general, adopt an even-handed foreign policy toward the Arabs and the Israelis. The true adoption of that policy by the United States and the West will certainly convince all skeptical persons and create a genuine dialogue between American/Western civilization and the Arab Muslim civilization. Following Obama's constructive address in Cairo to the Muslim world, many in the Arab Muslim world and outside of it have become rather optimistic about the achievement of a genuine solution to the Israeli-Palestinian conflict and, thus, to the larger Arab-Israeli conflict.

The Obama administration's realization of that would not be positively measured in political terms only but also in *cultural bonuses* which would make Americans closer to both the Arabs and the Muslims. Then, a positive attitude toward the United States today by over one billion and a half Arab Muslim population would be America's Mastercard to change its bad image of the Bush era for the better not only in the Arab Muslim world but over the entire world. Obama's leadership and his administration have not met this enormous challenge and put an end to the clash between America and the world at large. As argued in this work, *CS/ THD is the Basics of Basics to the process of civilization dialogue* whether between Islam and the West or between the USA and the rest of the world. The Obama administration's bargain was how to change for the better America's image in the Arab Muslim world and in the world at large. That required a positive and consistent solid action on the ground and soft and cleaver diplomacy framed in a good standing and articulate THD perspective. Because, without cultural understanding and respect for each other, human societies, nations, and civilizations are bound to *fail the real dialogue test* between them. Unfortunately, after Barack Obama, Donald Trump has worsened the relationship with the Arab World and Joe Bidden has not done better in favor of the establishment of the Palestinian state in the West Bank and Gaza. The policies of various American administrations in favor of Israel can be explained by our THD paradigm. There is more similarity in CS/ THD between Israel and the West than between it and the Arab Muslim World. *This deeply established THD difference* between the West and the Arabs and Muslims is a strong force that has shaped and will shape the nature of the relationship between them. That difference is a principal force behind the West's unconditional support for Israel. That is, the West's compelling favorable attitude toward Israel is not caused only by strategic geo-political reasons, but also and more likely by the West THD that favors the Jewish state and stands unfriendly to the Arab Muslim civilization. This attitude is *a green visa* for the continuation of the Clash of Civilizations. The West 's great support to Israel in Gaza crisis launched in October 2023 is highly influenced by the West's THD as stressed earlier. Multiples statements of official Western governments clearly express the nature of the West's THD led by Bidden administration. It is enough to mention only two political statements of the highest authorities in this administration: the President and the Secretary of State. In his visit to Israel in October 2023, Anthony Blinken has made this statement: "I come before you not only as the United States secretary of state but also as a Jew". He told this to an audience at Israel Defense Ministry at Tel Aviv. As to president Bidden, it is reported that he has said: "I have so long said: If Israel did not exist, we would have to invent it". These two declarations represent a Christian Jewish THD in opposition to an Arab Muslim THD. Their presence sets the scene for religious conflict between the West and the Arab Muslim World which is likely to extend the military confrontation in the region beyond Gaza and Israel. There is consensus worldwide that the solution to the Israeli – Palestinian conflict is *the establishment of two states* which is called for again and again including by Biden administration. The great support for this solution is based on *the principles of justice and fairness and humanism*: the Palestinian people is the only people in today world who is still under occupation.

References

Bochner, S. (editor1985) *Cultures in Contact*, Oxford, New York, Pergamon Press.

Dhaouadi, M. (2002) *Globalization of the Other Underdevelopment: Cultural Identities*, Kuala Lumpur, A. S Noordeen.

Dhaouadi, M. (2008) 'Arab Intellectual Concepts for Cultural Sociology, *Contemporary Arab Affairs*, I, I, 2008, 71–84.

Huntington, S. (1993) The Clash of Civilizations, *Foreign Affairs*, no. 72, Summer, excerpts in the book: *The Globalization Reader* edited by F. Lechner and J. Boli, Malden/USA, pp.36–43.

Newsweek Special Davos Edition Dec.2001–Feb.2002, p.9.

Saadi, M. (2006) *The Future of International Relations: From the Clash of Civilizations to the Humanization of Civilization and the Culture of Peace* (in Arabic) Beirut, Center for Arab Unity Studies.

Said, E. (1993) *Culture and Imperialism,* New York, Vintage.
White, L. (1973) *The Concept of Culture*, Edina, Alpha Editions.

www.ingramcontent.com/pod-product-compliance
Lightning Source LLC
Chambersburg PA
CBHW070657250726
48662CB00001B/168